AF480709

A TRUE STORY

Betrothed to
A Charlatan Preacher

There was Blood

By

VICINDA CRAWFORD

This book is designed to provide accurate and authoritative information regarding the subject matter covered. This information is given with the understanding that neither the author nor LEEDS PRESS CORP is engaged in rendering legal or professional advice. The opinions expressed by the author are not necessarily those of LEEDS PRESS CORP

Copyright 2022 © Leeds Press Corp

Cover copyright 2022 © Leeds Press Corp

Cover Design by Leeds Graphics.

Editorial by Leeds Press Corp

Written by Vicinda Crawford

Leeds Press Corp encourages the right to free expression and the importance of copyright. The objective of copyright is to encourage authors and artists to produce the innovative works that strengthens our society.

Betrothed to A Charlatan Preacher No part of this publication may be reproduced, stored in a retrieval system, or transmitted in any way by any means, electronic, mechanical, photocopy, recording or otherwise without the prior permission of the author except as provided by USA copyright law. If you would like permission to use material from the book (other than for review purposes), please contact info@leedspress.com. The opinions expressed by the author are not necessarily those of LEEDS PRESS CORP.

Leedspublishing.com

Table of Contents

Preface

It was on October 24th, 2017, when the Macon Telegraph. Reported this story in the newspaper. I vividly remember reading the article. The trial was over, and the guilty verdict had come in. Furthermore, a former pastor of a church in Macon, GA, had been sentenced to life in prison without the possibility of parole. Pastor William Pounds III appeared to read the Bible in court. He was accused of slaying his longtime girlfriend and fiancé, Ms. Kendra M. Jackson, in June of 2015. Kendra worked as a personal banker at the BB& T branch near the Macon Mall. I was the other fiancé. I had been questioned by the authorities, who had given me an account of everything that happened. I kept playing the tape in my head.

Was there any other way an innocent life could have been saved? They say that hindsight is 20/20, but mine was too foggy to piece together what remained of my life. I read articles and watched news on television. I was painted simply as the *other woman* from Atlanta that Mr. Pounds was also engaged to. Feelings of shame, depression, and nothingness overwhelmed me. I was betrothed to be married to this man. He had issues like everybody does. But how come he was engaged to two women? We all understand infidelity and extra-marital affairs but being engaged to a cold and calculating murderer was another story. To heal from the trauma, I have taken time away from everything and introspectively looked over my life from childhood. I have repeatedly played the tape of my life to see the gaps and failures in judgment. I live in fear of dating and trusting again. My life is forever changed.

I'm writing this book hoping that every woman who desires to get married can read and evaluate their own life and avoid the failures of judgment. I do not know that I could've seen the red flags, but maybe my own pain and loneliness got the best of me. As you read my story, I do not want to be a victim. I lived through it. My heart goes out to Kendra Jackson and her family. They lost a loving daughter and a God-fearing woman. All she ever wanted was a husband, a family, and a belonging. A woman's deepest desire and fulfillment in life is to belong.

I do not know why he spared me. Was I next? I do not know but what I do know is sociopaths and psychopaths are real. I have seen one, loved one, and temporarily lived with one. You must understand that they look very human, express emotions (fake), are great manipulators, wear great outfits, and even preach Sunday sermons. You may be living with one, related to one, and even loving one. You never know. Watch out, stay safe and investigate your own childhood and identify any vulnerabilities that could predispose you to such people. I have, and here is my story from my childhood until I found out my fiancé was a cold-blooded murderer.

"Mr. Pounds and I'm not gonna dignify you by calling you Rev. Pounds, you didn't earn that you are a liar, you are a manipulator, and frankly, you are an outright Charlatan."
- Bibb County Superior Judge Howard Z. Simms

Introduction

On September 6, 1967, I was born in Augusta, Georgia, to Virginia and Ollie Mills at Saint Joseph Hospital and grew up at 506 Dupont Street, the white house with blue seashell decorations. I am the second daughter born to my parents. My oldest sister and I have the same mother and father. I do have other siblings as well. Mom and my stepfather had two children, a boy, and a girl. My biological father had two boys from other marriages as well. It was a big family of biological and stepsiblings. We were raised in the same household. I was a little tomboy; I played in the neighborhood with my best friend, Annie. I remember being rough with every toy I got, and I damaged my bike by riding it through the bushes. I would climb and jump off houses and trees. In so many words I was not that kid that sat in the house and played with "girl toys" I was adventurous.

My mom and dad divorced when I was about three years old. I remember witnessing my first domestic violence incident when my dad physically assaulted my mother. He struck her with his fist, and she balled up in pain, covered her face. I saw her crawling around the house picking up her hair rollers, and I helped her pick them up. This was the first time she's ever told my grandfather about the abuse. As a result, her brothers (my uncles) taught my dad a lesson with some serious whoop-ass teachings. So he left our house and never came back and that led to a divorce. After the divorce, my mom, being a single parent, could not enroll me in our neighborhood elementary school. I had to go to my grandmother's house. That's how I enrolled at the local elementary school called Clara E Jenkins, where my grandmother lived in a small area called Hyde Park. A predominantly African American community. However, the school was located near chemical plants, and toxins emitted from them infected residents with cancer and other infections. That led to an uproar in the city, the issue made national news and the school was eventually closed.

Railroads tracks were close by I remember trains coming through while at school. It was always noisy. As crazy as I was, education was my stronger suit. I was an A and B student. I wore glasses. I was one of those kids who looked like they needed binoculars to see things. As expected, my schoolmates always made fun of me. When my glasses broke, I refused to wear new ones. I remember using a band-aid to tape them together. I even have a photo of me with the loosely taped glasses in one of my graduation photos. I laugh to this day at my stubborn self.

The tomboy in me was never afraid to walk home alone from school. One day I decided to walk home through some woods. Lo, behold, I saw Lisa, a girl I knew, being bullied by two other kids. They were chasing her. Thinking I was tough, I didn't hesitate to intervene. I recall pushing the two kids, attacking her, and kicking them off her. I helped Lisa get up from the ground and told her to run home and tell her mother. I was screaming as loud as I could as we both ran home.

Many people in my grandmother's neighborhood were scared of my uncles. They were known for their toughness and ability to fight. My uncles used to teach me how to box. They'd put gloves on my hands, and we would practice boxing. They wanted me to be tough. They believed that in our neighborhood, you had to defend yourself. It didn't matter if you were a boy or girl. We also target practiced using shotguns. Then my mom met my stepfather, who was in the military. He moved into our house off Dupont Street. I'm not sure how long we were there. He was an officer in the military and very strict. And that's when my world changed. We had a playroom full of toys, and my stepfather did not want us to play too much. He was strict with education. So, he took our toys except for two, put them up on a pickup truck, and drove away with them. Don't know where he took them. But my little world was shuttered with when my toys were taken away.

I could've survived, but then he took my favorite dune buggy too. I loved that thing; I drove it so fast and made perfect circles with it. My little heart was broken. I still look for this dune buggy to this day. I will do anything to get it back. It was my best friend and protection, an escape from the chaotic world. And that was just the start. The next thing I knew, we were moving to a military base. I could not find my footing. My little world was falling apart. In the new home, everything had to be clean. I remember him wearing a white glove and swiping on the windowpanes of the room to ensure it was squeaky clean. If he found dust, we did the cleaning all over. My stepfather loved golf. I remember him teaching us how to play the game behind our house.

When we went to court, my last name changed from Mills to Crawford. We were legally his children now. So, we left the state of Georgia shortly after the name change. I couldn't understand why my biological father changed our names at that time. Later, I heard through the grapevine that my mother had threatened my biological father with outstanding child support if he objected to the name change. Even with the name change, I maintained my relationship with my father's family. I was around my dad's side of the family all the time. It was fascinating that I loved being around my father's family but not him. It was a weird dynamic. I guess when they say that blood is thicker than water its true.

When we moved to a military base in Fort Leavenworth, Kansas, I was ten years old. It was also the first time I attended a predominantly Caucasian school. I was devasted when my grades plummeted to a C average. Up to that point, I had been an A and B student. Our family dynamic had changed. I withdrew from being an extrovert. I kept more to myself. Always afraid of getting whippings for not cleaning the house. I hardened myself and grew cold on the inside. Never showed my emotions. I remember one time my stepfather whipped me so badly, but I refused to cry. He kept whipping me, but I held my breath until my nose bled. When he stopped, I ran out of the room and cleaned my nose with a towel. Things continued to shift and change in our household, domestic squabbles ensued. I remember seeing my mother and my stepfather getting into it. My older sister pulled out a knife on him to defend my mother. The military police came and removed him from our house temporarily for a few weeks. Things never stayed the same as our family was getting torn apart.

In school, I developed a liking for sports. Until field day at school, I didn't realize how fast I could run track. I won every race. The coach said, "Do you realize how fast you are?" And I'm like, "No, I never ran track before." I just ran around in the neighborhood. He signed me up for the track and field program. Sports became my safe space away from the issues at home. My stepfather returned, after they had done some counseling with the military programs.

My mother enrolled me in other programs as well. I joined the Jazz, tap, and ballet classes. I even became a girl scout. All these extra-curriculum activities helped me develop social skills. Our neighbor had two children, a son, and a girl. I used to play with them at their house. Life was difficult at home but bearable because of my new connections with other kids my age. During the summer, I would visit my cousins in New Jersey. I remember my stepfather working at the Pentagon and going for extended periods. Their relationship had deteriorated over the years. There were more fights than earlier on in Kansas. At one point, I remember my mother, my siblings, and I living temporarily in New Jersey. It was during that time that mom broke the news of being pregnant. Shortly after, my stepfather was transferred to California, so we relocated to California.

In California, I joined a new school and resumed my love for sports. I played softball on top of the track and field. It was in California that I encountered racism because of my skin color. I was called Blackie, Four-eyes, Ugly, Boney, and Skinny. I learned a lot and matured rapidly because of circumstances. It was in California that I first experienced an earthquake. I saw things moving and cabinets shaking in the house. It was not a pleasant experience. I had no control and nowhere to go. It lasted for a few minutes, but those minutes felt like forever.

I started babysitting for the first time outside of my own siblings. He was a three-year-old son of a Three-Star General in the Army; they were Caucasian. They trusted me with their precious son because I followed their instructions to the T. She wrote down instructions. He must have told his mom that he liked me because it became my permanent job after school, giving me another outlet. I spent a lot of time at their home, and they treated me very nicely. I would walk to their house, and they just trusted me. I was never afraid to go over there.

On the family front, my mother's pregnancy developed a complication. I was worried for her life. Thank God things worked out. I remember we had a malfunctioning light at the house. One day while my parents were out at the Officer's Country Club for breakfast, my sister playing with a balloon, accidentally hit the bulb. The whole thing came down and fell on my head. One of the pieces broke on my arm, and blood came shooting out of my vein. In horror and fear, I screamed. We had no cellphones to call in an emergency back in the day. I have a scar on my arm to this day. Leaving Veronica, one of my best friends in California, was true heartbreak. We relocated to Pennsylvania and were stationed at Fort Indiantown Gap, near Annville. This area was known as the Quakers community. We attended a Baptist Church, and I also joined Northern Lebanon High School. I was called the "N" at this school. On a piece of paper, a white girl said, "For Sale, anyone wants to buy an N...er," That piece of paper got to me after being passed around the class. I was devastated.

The principal made her apologize to me. The teachers were very forthcoming. They didn't allow that nonsense in their classrooms. It wasn't something they swept under the rug. The principal didn't allow racism in his school either. We had a few blacks at the school. I remember the boys playing football for the school as well. They were well-loved and accepted by most of the school community. We rode on the same bus to school. However, one day a white guy on the bus stood up and started calling the brothers "N" word. One of the brothers snatched the boy by his shirt, pulling him over the school bus seat. The bus driver pulled to the side; we were all on the bus in shock to see what was going on, but he snatched him up and said, "You will never call me that name again!" It scared so many people. Students suddenly wanted to hang out with me and be friends. He set a precedent on the bus and in school. It must have gotten around, or maybe that white guy was the biggest bully at the school. But it changed the dynamic of how I was received there. It was interesting, and I listened to more rock and roll music.

I remember being ridiculed by my cousins when I started listening to Rock and Roll music. They were like,

"Now you are a little white girl?" I knew what they meant. I was not listening to black music like they did. But that was ok by me. All I wanted was to join the track and field program. But because the policy required that I be in 10th or higher, I joined basketball instead. I played point guard for the basketball team. I was only 5' 5,' but I could outjump the girls from the other teams. My grades took a hit at this school, but I managed to stay positive.

The school had various activities for the student. I joined the graphic design class, other students joined wood classes, etc. The church we attended was predominantly Quakers. I was assigned a female mentor. She was nice to me and treated me like her own daughter. I fell in love with reading books. They had Christian books for teenagers, and I read all of them. I didn't realize I had a passion for reading. But that became my hobby.

My family relocated again to Atlanta, Georgia. I had become accustomed to the military lifestyle of always moving from one place to another. I kept up with my grades in school through all this. My sister and I shared a room. Our parents expected us to keep it clean. It was not unreasonable at all. The issue was my sister did not care that we did. To avoid too much trouble and punishment from our parents, I cleaned the room all by myself most of the time. I developed an obsessive-compulsive disorder O. C. D. over the years. My side of the room was very clean because I was afraid of getting in trouble, and my sister didn't care. She just threw things all over the place. My parents always said if the entire room wasn't clean, you're both in trouble. I would clean her side of the room. We always had chores; she would be rebellious and not complete her chores because she wanted to live with my biological father. It was her way of demanding that my dad's family be included in our lives.

My grades in high school slowly began to improve back to As and Bs in my senior year. I was able to run track and field at Southwest Dekalb High school. My high school track and field career changed my life. I obtained the title of the fastest girl at my school in the 100-yard dash and 220-yard dash. I ran the last leg on the 440-yard relay team. I also trained and competed in the long jump. I ran track and field during my school and summer track seasons. I worked hard on my grades and talent to ensure I received a full-ride scholarship. My coach helped me learn and do the basics needed to obtain a collegiate scholarship.

I remember being very resentful to my parents when I found out they were divorcing. I did not want them at my events because they only reminded me of the family that I once had. In the back of my mind, they were leaving each other. It really hurt and affected my performance. I lost one of my favorite races when I came in second. Their divorce affected my concentration. Overall, I won Most Valuable Player, Women of the Year, and was named the fastest in the State of Georgia. My high school record stood for 20 years. After graduating from high school, I ran my last summer track season; I only competed in the long jump because of my injury. Jumping my personal best of 20 feet and won the AAU championship in the event. I wanted a full-ride scholarship to college. I received several phone calls from different colleges. My parents were so focused on ending their marriage and not helping me.

I started dating in High School. My boyfriend played a trick on me by pretending that he was a college coach calling from a college to offer me a scholarship. I was excited, and then he laughed, and it hurt my soul, but I was so mad at him. I had the grades, the talent, and I couldn't understand why he played that trick on me. My summer coach worked with Georgia Tech's track program. He knew that I wanted to get the scholarship and was willing to help me if I worked on my skills and kept in shape. As fate would have, my boyfriend and I were active sexually. I found out that I was pregnant, which killed my scholarship ambitions. I was not a virgin when I met my boyfriend. I had this secret of being sexually abused during my younger years. I remember the sexual abuse that happened at my grandmother's house. Back in those days, people never spoke about such matters. So, I kept it myself. He never penetrated me, but he rubbed his body part on mine. He was a teenager; I guess it was hormones flying...

I told a family member that he was touching me inappropriately; no police were called back then. Not sure what happened to him because he was still around the house when I got out of school. I sometimes ran away from my grandmother's house because I didn't want to be around him.

One day I got into an argument with my aunt at my grandmother's house, who wasn't that much older than me, and I ran away. Walking on Gordon Highway by myself was not safe. I remember this man, a perfect stranger pulling by my side and asking where I was going, what my name and my parents' names were. I did not want to engage a stranger, so I ran but could not go too far. He followed me closely and begged that I trust him and he would not hurt but take me home safely. After the back and forth, I trusted him. And he kept his promise and drove me home to my parent. My mother was extremely upset with me for running away from my grandmother's house.

God protected me that day. I didn't know the level of danger I put myself in and worrying my grandmother. My mom did not know I ran away until that man told her the story of where he had located me. I survived the incident.

My first crush on a boy was when I was 12 years old. During the summer, I visited my cousin in New Jersey, his name was Edward, but Edward didn't like me. He called me names like Blackie, ugly, and four eyes because of my thick glasses. They were all running around and laughing at me. But everybody knew I liked him, and he knew it too. Every summer, I would visit my cousin Pam. We are five months apart, and people call us twins; however, she is the pretty twin. I would see Edward, but it did not hurt because my crush was on this white guy at my school in Pennsylvania. I think my friends told him, but I remember him asking me to dance at our fall school dance. He had long blond hair, like one of the rock n roll groups. I had not kissed a boy at this point; he was just another crush.

When I moved to Georgia, I had my first teenage crush, losing my virginity. We were both virgins and teenage nerds. It only happened one time. I was too scared to do anything again. I was like, if this is all there is to it, I don't want to do it again. Then I met Brent Nelson, my daughter's father; I had the biggest crush on him. He ran track. I ran track. Everybody knew I liked him. I took advanced classes with him. I would see him in the hallway at his locker and dream of being my boyfriend. I thought he was so cute. He was a light complexion, with a little bitty head, but a jokester. He had that personality of not being afraid. Everybody laughed at his crazy jokes, and he was very athletic. I compared him to the singer Morris Day. I had a crush on Morris Day. He had the same energy and stuff. I just fell for him. I was developing a good friendship with my new best friend Winona, who lived down the street, and I was like, girl, he is so cute. Oh, but I think he has a girlfriend. His girlfriend had light eyes; she was cool. So even on the track, I could hear guys saying that I was so fast. He took a liking to me when my popularity soared. He did ask my dad permission to take me out on a date. This was our first date. Everybody was shocked to see us at the basketball game. I was so shy I remember writing down my talking points before he called me. I was so shy. He thought I was a virgin, but I wasn't. I think in his eyes, he was getting another virgin. He talked me into sneaking out with him in the night. He told me that he was now my boyfriend, and I should know what he thought was best. His parents were not there, and that's how we started having sex. Even though I heard rumors of him being with other girls, I kept a low profile to avoid friction and losing him.

I had low self-esteem from being teased by other kids about my skin color and wearing glasses. So, Brent made me feel secure enough to start wearing them again to school. My best friend Winona always told me I was beautiful because of my skin color. She would trade my skin with her paperback color skin. Winona had my back no matter what. She could fight and curse you out in a blink of an eye. Her family moved to Georgia from Boston when she was younger. The other new girl on the track could run very fast in the 100, 200-yard dash, the hurdles. She was a star-long jumper as well. She jumped 21.4 feet in high school. She was beautiful and attractive. Guys at school were attracted to her. We became friends and got to know her family. She told me I was pretty and showed me how-to put-on makeup. She showed me how to dress better and stylishly. I started wearing makeup daily. I had long, thick, wild hair, and my father wouldn't let me get a perm. I wore it big and puffy. Other guys started noticing me and giving me compliments. I did not care about them, only Brent. He had one sister, and they frequently argued. One day it got so heated he physically beat her. And that was my first cue, not to argue or disagree with him. I feared violence.

I had to stay the good girl, you do what he says, you be nice, you're a good girl. Do not look at any other boys and make sure he didn't think I was ever cheating on him. I found out after high school how many guys wanted to talk to me, but they knew not to even bother because of him. He graduated a year before me and moved to New York with his dad. However, we're supposed to be still dating. I could not date anybody else. It was my assumption he might have been dating someone else. I don't know, but I knew I would stay true to him. I did not date anyone, and I did not go to the prom with anyone else. He didn't come, and he was supposed to come down, and then at the last minute, he couldn't; my dad wouldn't let him come. He didn't want him to come. Still, I stayed true to him. When it was time for me to graduate, I was going to college; he came back home, and there it was. I hadn't had sex. September 10 was right after my birthday. I know that was the day I got pregnant.

Even though we were dating, I still feared him. I had seen enough domestic abuse in my own family and him hitting his sister. I didn't want the same to happen to me. Before Brent, I had lost my virginity. After that encounter, it felt like we were perfect strangers when we met. No emotional connections, none whatsoever. My experience with dating was not pleasant. I didn't get to go out on dates other than sex and meet at school.

Chapter 1

I've blocked out a lot of stuff in my childhood, but I believe my mom went through a lot after her first divorce. I had a feeling of being tossed aside. My mother was a very clean and organized person. She worked hard to make ends meet as a single parent. She was not the hugger or showed a lot of affection. I just started to fend for myself, trying to be strong, knowing my mom was a single parent. My sister spent most of her time at our grandmother's house. I felt accepted when doing something athletic such as track and field, basketball, cheerleader, and soccer. Besides that, l felt like I didn't exist in my family. As I mentioned in my introduction, my mother remarried, and we moved to the military base. It was a different experience for my sister and me.

My church was preparing for a Christmas Play at a local theatre. I had been assigned a character in the play and had a line to recite. My sister and I were cast to play on several screens as extras. I remember being overwhelmed. The producer wanted me to read the line as loud as possible. Tears wanted to form, but I was accustomed to hiding in a safe place when I cried. The words I had to say to Jesus as I grabbed the hem of his garment were, "Jesus, please read me a story." At first, the words would not come out because I was scared. I mumbled the line. Not being loud enough, the producers pushed me to the side, and my line was given to another girl who recited them loudly. That was all they did. I was not given a chance to work on my vocal cords. I was humiliated and crushed before other kids. I felt like a failure. At that point, I felt like my life was meant to be seen and not to be heard. I kept to myself.

I went through school wanting to speak up. I became quiet and reserved. When I raised my hand in class, it was as though the teacher overlooked me. I could read and pronounce my words well, so what was the problem? I struggled with my appearance in school, and I think most kids picked up on those vulnerabilities.

My mother had a son that she always wanted to make matters worse. So, I felt like I was not wanted or needed and had to fend for myself. And that's how track and field became my escape from my dark and negative reality.

My older sister ran track and field as well. I set up a goal to beat her in the 100-meter dash, and when I finally did, she was mad at me. To avoid conflict, I tempered down my athletic abilities and allowed her to win just so there would be peace. I did this in so many activities. I allowed people to outshine me just they would feel better than me. I didn't know it was a psychological issue to deal with.

I remember when the announcer called for all long jump athletes to report to the long jump pit. It was my turn to run down the runway to mark my steps, making sure I hit the board and leap into the pit without going over the foul line. Everything was set, and I stepped onto the runway to make my first jump of six. We had six attempts to make your longest jump. In my head, I was replaying all the exercises and techniques my coach had practiced with me for the last two weeks. I started off with three long strides, then full out sprint down the runway; without looking down, I planted my right foot on the board and sailed into the air uncontrollably. I felt free and flying so high, unable to control my body. Once all the dirt cleared, the white flag raised to indicate the jump was good, and the digital sign flashed 20'0 feet. My longest jump ever and gold medalist for the AAU championship. That was one of the memorable occasions when I didn't think about other people. I was in the zone.

I put other people's desires and wants before mine for a long time. I had become comfortable playing second fiddle. But this feeling of inadequacy slowly ate at my soul. Everything in me was screaming, "why not me?" I, too, mattered. I longed for acknowledgment and validation. But none came my way. So, sports became my outlet. In my relationship with Brent, I just let him have his way in most instances, even though I had my own opinions and reservations. I had adopted a layback mindset. I would give other people accolades, but no one cared to do the same for me. I remember my boyfriend telling me that in the bible, it said that you do unto others as you would wish to be done to you. The only problem was that I did unto others, but mine never came to me!

I was hidden in plain sight. I never wanted my mom to know I was crying a lot. I wanted her to be happy. She knew that I wanted to go to my now deceased aunt and uncle's house to spend time with my favorite cousin Pam in New Jersey in the summertime. This made me very happy. My body was changed from running track each year, and the New Jersey guys started noticing me. They asked my cousin, "Where's your country cousin with the little waist, the big booty, the nice running legs. I always thought, okay, that's a compliment, but they looked at me sexually, not as a potential girlfriend. I don't think it was the proper attention, but it was some type of attention. Finally, I was noticed as cute as opposed to being book smart. I would hear you are pretty for a dark or chocolate girl. Not you are pretty. The guys that called me ugly, dark, and four-eyed looked at me differently. My cousin lived in the same place I had my first crush at twelve years old. In the summer of 1985, after I graduated from high school and won the long jump in the AAU Track and Field championship, I was gifted a trip to New Jersey by my mom. The person I had a crush on all those years saw my cousin sitting outside on the porch with me. My crush called my cousin over to his car to talk. My cousin called me over to the car, and my crush said I didn't recognize you. For the first time in five years, he told me I was beautiful. His compliment made me smile so hard. Later that day, I was outside taking pictures with my cousin, having a great time. I was so small from running track that I didn't wear a bra most of the time. We took some cute pictures. I couldn't wait to show my boyfriend when I returned to Georgia. Well, my boyfriend, my first daughter's father, saw the picture and immediately said, you didn't have a bra on. I replied, what are you talking about? I didn't have to wear a bra, and he went off on me. He said the picture was distasteful. I was coming out of my shell, my crush called me a beautiful track running body, and I was eighteen years old. The picture was not distasteful to me. He could only pick out I didn't have a bra on. You called me a hoe just because I didn't have a bra on. I felt so bad; it made me think my body was ugly. I started wearing bigger clothes. I realized it didn't matter because guys noticed me. He body shamed me is how I took it. I would start really covering up more because I didn't want attention. I was a sexy eighteen-year-old girl, proud of my body, but I had to hide it. He controlled the clothes I wore when I was with or without him. I couldn't go to my dad about this because my parents were going through a divorce. I was even nervous about my track uniform. Even though he ran track, I didn't even want him at the track meets. I literally took my uniform sweatpants off at the last minute. I had to wear my hair long. My dad wouldn't allow me to cut my hair. I was afraid to get my eyebrows arched. I don't think I wore makeup until my 11th-grade year. One of my grandmothers was a Seventh Day Adventist. The other one was Jehovah's Witness and trying to maneuver between the two religions at a young age was confusing. My mom attended a Baptist church. The restriction helped my confusion with my boyfriend's demand for my clothing and hair. The Seventh Day Adventist church did not allow me to wear earrings or makeup. My body image was negative. I would beat myself up. I wanted to be this sexy girl because I saw my friends wearing what I considered sexy. However, I started getting the wrong attention and thinking he would like me more if I had sex with the guy. That was the furthest thing from the truth. They're going to respect you when you say no. But I didn't even respect myself. So why would I say no to them? Why did I do everything they asked me to do but didn't have demands of what I wanted from them. If they told me to wear my hair long, I wore my hair long. I referred to my childhood when my dad told me I could not cut my hair. I dated a guy who wanted my hair natural and short. What did I do? Yes, I cut it all off into a natural style. Personally, I love a short haircut. I don't think I had my own identity. It was always what they demanded out of me. I grew up in the deep south, how the parents and grandparents and any adult, you, no matter what, respect all adults. I think I lost respect for myself from all the demands. I can't pinpoint when I was truly happy other than on the track in my childhood.

Chapter 2

I was 18 years old, finished high school, and can't remember the exact date I found out. I told my boyfriend, Brent, of my pregnancy. He suggested I have an abortion. I didn't have any money for an abortion, and my mind was concentrating on running track in college. I was training with my track coach and had to tell him I was pregnant. I remember seeing the disappointment on his face. He knew I would excel in college and on the track. I relied on him; he kept saying he would get the money. I did tell my mother. Mom was sad, and I disappointed her. My mom was married early and had my sister and me by twenty-one. However, she was married, and that was the difference. I was embarrassed about being pregnant out of wedlock. The church members were expecting me to leave for college and run track. His sister and mom were very nice to me. However, I never knew how his father received the pregnancy. Now he was like, it's my fault that he can't go to college. I kept encouraging him to go to college because he was astute academically. He had already joined the US Marine Corp as a Reservist. But he kept coming up with excuses not to go to college. During my pregnancy, I started receiving phone calls and hearing rumors that Brent saw other women. He was living his life. I went to all my doctor's appointments with my mom or myself. My doctor's last name was Crawford, and he delivered at Crawford Long Hospital in Atlanta, GA. He was a very nice doctor. Physically I was in great shape because I was still running and training up to the third month of my pregnancy. I was healthy without any physical complications. The emotional relationship with him was the most challenging part of my pregnancy. He would guilt me by saying that I was ruining his life. He wasn't taking me to the doctors or supporting me. At this point, he will be around after she is born and stop dealing with other women. As it got closer to my due date, he started coming around and calling me as if he cared. He wanted to be instrumental in naming our baby. We went back and back and forth about her name and finally agreed on a name. On June 9, I went into labor with contractions 10 minutes apart. I was only two centimeters dilated, but the doctor didn't send me home; they had me walking up and down the halls. After hearing so many other people experience having sex during pregnancy, I decided not to have sex, which meant this was my first baby. Everything was going to be tight'. I was afraid it was going to be a complicated delivery. After 20 hours of labor, I still was less than 5 centimeters dilated. I was doing everything the doctor was telling me to do. The pain kicked in. The contractions were 5 minutes apart, and it was only my mom there; he still was not there. I had already been in labor for 26 hours. Finally, I was 5 centimeters, but the pain got worst. The nurse told me I could get the epidural because

I was dilating. My labor progressed quickly after the epidural because I started throwing up. Prepping to move to the delivery room, he shows up to see his daughter's birth; after pushing two times, on June 10, 1986, at 5:20 am, she was here, Cortney Djene' Nelson. She was white and very tiny. She was rushed out of the delivery room because she was jaundiced. He left the hospital, and I didn't see him for three days until the day of my discharge. I tried to move my legs, but I couldn't. I was petrified, not realizing the epidural temporarily paralysis your lower extremities. Dr. Crawford was discharging me. My baby had only urinated, and since she didn't have a bowel movement, I would have to leave her there. I started thinking somebody would kidnap my child. What did I do wrong? I thought maybe it was the epidural, and naturally, I should have toughed it out. I could not find the heart to leave my baby. I remember calling him crying; they won't release her because she needs to have a bowel movement; I'm on my way up there. Brent showed up, rocking our baby and having a personal conversation. Soon afterward, she had her first bowel movement, and we were discharged from the hospital together. I wanted to breastfeed, but she would not latch on, and she was crying a lot. I started beating myself up like, see, I told you are not a good mother. I did experience postpartum. Thinking, how am I going to do this? I'm 18 years old; I don't have a job. I refuse to get on any government assistance outside

Medicaid, which paid for her birth. I was happy thinking now maybe he will, you know, go to work and take care of our daughter. He did not stay active in her life. He continued to date other women. She cries all the time, exactly like I did during my pregnancy. She woke up every 2 hours with a piercing scream. My mom did step in to help as much as possible. Some nights she closed her door, and I had to deal with the screams by myself; lesson learned. One day, I recall he came over to pick her up and take her to see his family. She was about two or three months old. I was emotional about this day; however, I would let her go with her father. I packed her diaper and milk bag and had enough bottles for the day. When he brought her back, I looked at her bottles, and they were all full of milk from early. I asked him if he had purchased milk, and his response was she wasn't hungry? Do you know what happened after that? Yes, a bad argument. I gave him a second chance to spend time with her. When he arrived, I didn't recognize the vehicle he was driving. He told me it was his girlfriend's car, and my response was, you're not taking her in your female car. I went against my word. I was an emotional teenager on this day, and I didn't care. We get into a big argument. My daughter was already in the car, and he tried to back up and pull out of the driveway while the car was moving; I reached in, attempting to grab the keys. He kept driving, ran after him, jumped into the driver's window to stop him, turned the car off, took the keys, and threw the keys in the yard. I grabbed my daughter and her baby bag out of the backseat, and I went back into the house and closed the door. He found his keys and left my home. Don't ever disrespect me by bringing some bitch's car over here to pick up my daughter; you have a car or access your parents' car. Please don't do that, primarily since you didn't feed her last time. Things were getting hard for me, and I didn't know what to do. When my daughter was six months, my aunts, Rosalind and Nora, on my biological father's side of the family, said, if you are in college and working, we will help you. My daughter went to Augusta with my aunts for months before moving there, and I started college. I was working at Macy's Department store. I decided to move to Augusta permanently and raise my daughter there. I was doing very well, my daughter was two years old, and her father was trying to ease his way back into my life, but I wouldn't allow him. I met someone six years older than me who was pleasant. This man was a father of a six-year-old girl and a manager of the Champs Sporting Goods store at the mall. I was walking in Regency Mall with my daughter, he was at work, and he ran out into the hallway to stop me. I turned around, looking at him, saying to myself; He's not trying to talk to me. I am a teenage mom. That was the first thing that came to my mind, but he had asked me for my phone number and complimented me about my hair. I had long, thick hair; he said my hair was beautiful. He wanted to know if he could take me out for lunch and get to know me. I gave him my number, and he did follow up with me. I was thinking, is this what you consider typical dating. He got to know my daughter and my family. We started dating, and this made my daughter's father nervous. My guy told me that if you stay in college, finish college, I got you, and take care of your daughter. I was afraid to be with someone like that, and I didn't know why, but he was what I needed in my life. I didn't think I was good enough for this remarkable man. I pushed him away as nobody treats me like that; you're not supposed to be good to me or give me these things. He ended up meeting my mom, and my mom liked him. She tried to keep us together. I would have welcomed this type of man in my life now and avoided a lot of heartaches. My stepsister was driving, and I was in the passenger seat when she noticed the guy driving a grey vehicle next to us. He pointed for us to pull over. He was the true meaning of tall, dark, and handsome. He reminded me of my favorite singer, Keith Sweat. I thought he was approaching my stepsister, but he wanted my name and phone number. I hesitated to give him my phone number because I was on a break from dating and focusing on college and work. He was in the Marine Corp. We exchanged information. We went out for several months, traveling and spending time at what I thought was his apartment or at my house. I sent him a birthday card with my aunt's address. One morning my aunt picked me up heading to work; she told me they had a visit at their home from a lady who stated she was George's wife. My heart dropped. At 19 years old, I had never been with a married man and didn't know how to turn off my feelings. This man did things to me I had never experienced. I confronted him, and he told the truth. He said they were on a break, and she refused to give him a baby. He was leaving her. I tried to continue the relationship. It was too much, and hurting another female, so we ended it. One evening my stepsister and I decided to hang out at the NCO club on the military base at Fort Gordon, GA. We were allowed to drink on base at 18 years old. After a couple of drinks, a sexy paper sack brown skin, 6'5, with bowlegs man asked me to dance. His last name was Stocky; he drove a drop-top black Camaro. After we started dating, he gave me a set of keys to his vehicle and apartment. Everything was going great until I went out with the girls. We went to the same NCO club, but I did not dance with anyone or exchange phone numbers because I was in a relationship with him. He called me and accused me of being all up on some guy. He had a friend telling him this information. He described clothing that I did not own. We took pictures that night, and I was willing to show them to him. We argued, and he accused me of cheating, and I was hurt. Two weeks later, I received a phone call from my stepsister asking if I knew Stocky was at the NCO club tonight. She described the outfit I purchased as a gift for him earlier that week. He told me he was home. She said she spoke to him. I made several phone calls which he didn't answer. Later the next day, he answered the phone, saying he was coming to the house. He was in the outfit described, denied speaking to my stepsister, going out to the club, and was extremely tired. I didn't press it because I knew he was lying. With the relationship issues, school expenses, and a low-paying job, I decided it was time for something else. I wanted to join the United States Marine Corp because George spoke highly about it. The Marines were physically challenging, paying for my college, making enough money to raise my daughter, and stability. I wanted a career, not a job. Being in a relationship with a married man and the situation with my last boyfriend was embarrassing and the last straw. I had a fantastic recruiter who was honest about my process of getting through Marine Bootcamp. I left for the United States Marine Corps on December 5, 1988. I signed temporary custody of my daughter to my aunt Nora. US Marine Corps boot camp was challenging, exciting, and life-changing, pushing your mind and body to another level. On March 8, 1989, I graduated and received orders to Fort Benjamin Harrison, IN, for postal training. I love the military family. I met Marines, Naval, Army, and Air Force brothers and sisters. I wasn't trying to date anyone. However, I learned how to order and drink more than two mixed drinks in one night. I did not have sex with anyone, and we treated each other as family. I completed my training in three weeks and received my official orders. I was off to Okinawa, Japan, to start my tour of duty. I was missing my daughter so much. I will be gone for a year from her and my family. I am doing this for us, and it will get easier. After receiving my tax refund, my daughter was set up financially with my aunts. I flew out to California, received my orders, and boarded the military plane with hundreds of Marines and fighter tanks. I met another female Marine named Kourtney on the aircraft. I was like, wow, my daughter's name is Cortney. We departed California on a Wednesday and arrived in Okinawa, Japan, on Friday due to the time zone differences. During my first few days in Japan, I met Tam, and I was still hanging out with Kourtney as we both were adjusting to the climate and assignment. After sleeping off the jet lag, I decided to walk around outside when I woke up. I noticed a handsome guy sitting at the guard desk. I was a new female marine on base. I arrived late in the evening in full uniform with my hair pulled in a bun. My hair was out of the bun and long, flowing down my back. You have beautiful long hair; then he takes his hat off and rubs his hands through his hair. Yes, I'm black and Indian as he gives me this look and smile. He states, you and another female just got here. I answered, yes, sir. He replied you don't have to call me, sir. I'm just a Marine like you. He asked, do you have a boyfriend? Yes, I have a boyfriend. He replied with a smile; well, he's back in America. We'll see how long that lasts. I said, but I have a best friend; you can talk to her. Okay, well, what's her number? I wrote to my best friend, telling her about him and how things were going. The conversation continued when my girl Tam walked up, telling me he was a good guy from Philly like her, and they were friends. On Tuesday, I learned about bosses' night at the NCO club. We had to purchase a drink for our boss. Tam, Kourtney, and I attended bosses' night, and I had several inexpensive drinks. Marines were buying drinks for us instead. I think I had at least ten drinks. The night went by quickly as we drank and danced; we all left the NCO club stumbling and could barely walk back to the barracks. When I made it back to my room, it was people everywhere. I am not sure who my roommates were or the guys in our room. They were drinking, lying on my bunk, and doing other stuff. I didn't want to stay in the room. I walked to Tam's room and told her what was happening inside my room. I will be outside on the bench, sobering up and getting some fresh air. I was outside for about ten or fifteen minutes when I felt an arm around my shoulder. He asked if I was okay. It was Calvin from the guard desk I met earlier. We sat outside and talked before he walked me back to my room, but I couldn't find my key. I would sleep on the floor in Tam's room, but I think her boyfriend was there. I had nowhere to go; I'll let you sleep in my room. I won't do anything, and he did not. He was nice and respectful to me. We started hanging out with his friends. By the time my best friend received the letter, I had liked him for myself. Stocky wanted to make things work right before I left for Japan; I said he was my boyfriend. I wrote him a letter when I wrote my best friend, and he never wrote back. I was officially Calvin's girlfriend, and things were going great. Because of my job assignment, I was moved to another base closer to the main post office. He made every effort to come to see me. I was in a true relationship. He was the second guy to treat me like a princess. He was very protective, and we spent a lot of time together. He was an only child and extremely close to his mom. Calvin sent her money every month just because he wanted to. Most women were dating multiple men because the ratio was 1 to 200. I was only dating him, and he knew it. One night Tam, Kourtney, and I went out to a different NCO club, and Calvin was happy I was hanging with my girls. I decided I only had one drink, enjoying the music and chill. I was standing around sipping on my drink when a guy asked me for a dance. I politely declined because I was only chilling tonight. He kept asking and began to get loud. I walked away, and he screamed at me. You are nothing but a BITCH anyways. That's when my girls jumped in, going off on him. The security guards removed him from the club. We left the club and went to Calvin's room to tell him what had happened. Calvin wanted to know if I was okay and the best description of the guy. Within a couple of days, he located the guy, and he apologized for calling me out by my name. In July, I found out I was pregnant with my second child. When I told Calvin, he told me I better not kill his child. Abortion was not an option. The difference between my first and second pregnancies was that he was more protective and made sure I was okay. He went with me to the doctor's appointments. I was very sick and throwing up a lot. He was always trying to find something I could eat and not be nauseous. Still, all the different smells of Okinawa, Japan, and pregnant made me sick. About two months into my pregnancy, a big event was happening at the beach, and Calvin wanted me to attend it with him. I wasn't feeling well, and I told him to go without me. He was reluctant to leave me behind, but I convinced him to have some fun. Well, I started getting worse, and the pain in my stomach intensified. I decided to go to the guard desk for help. I need to go to the hospital. He was trying to find a taxicab because everybody who had cars was at the beach. I was standing outside looking for a taxicab when a group of Marines returned to the barracks because they needed to pick up something and then return to the beach. Are you okay? I'm not. Can you drop me off at the hospital? They said yes, come on; we'll drop you off at the hospital. We all squeezed into this little car. I'm in the emergency room. The emergency doctor checked me and could not figure out why I was in so much pain. He said the baby looked good. He decided to have the OB/GYN doctor check before discharging me, who conducted a test based on my symptoms. I moved back into the exam room, where he inserted a long needle with a tube attached to my uterus. The tube immediately began to fill up with blood. I was bleeding internally from a ruptured cyst, and I had emergency surgery. He told me it was a strong possibility I would lose my baby. He asked, Can I reach the father? I told the nurse he was on the beach for the event. I gave my supervisor, Sgt. B. Wilson, information, and she knew the father. Sgt. Wilson called me at the hospital, and I informed her of my condition. She said, don't worry, I will find him. I changed my clothes; the IV started in my arm, the anesthesiologist prepped me, and the doctor prepared to operate on me. The thought of losing my baby continued to fill my mind, not seeing and telling Calvin what was going on. He kept saying he wanted to stay with me, but I wanted him to enjoy the beach. The room started spinning around. Sgt. Wilson made it to the hospital in time to tell me she was working on locating Calvin. I was prepped for surgery and pushed down the hallway; my bed hit the operation room doors when I heard his voice scream my name. He hugs and kisses me and tells me we will be fine. It felt like I was in a movie, but this was my real life happening. The operating room was a cold, dark, and old-school setup. I fell asleep, thinking my baby would be gone when I woke up. The first thing the nurse said to me when I opened my eyes was, you baby is still here. We could get to the ruptured cyst and stop the bleeding, but the next two weeks will determine if your baby survives because the bleeding was bad. He was there with me the entire time. My roommates Barb Holdman and Didi Gonzales took me back to my barracks and waited on me hand and foot. My baby survived past the two-week mark. I had a man in my life who genuinely cared about me. He did little things to show me how much he cared about me. We went to the beach, and I was pregnant; he would pick me up and carry me. If you don't put me down, he's like, nope, you said your feet are tired, I'm going to carry you. Everything in the relationship and pregnancy was beautiful until he received his military orders to his next duty station in California. My entire world turned upside down because it was nothing I could do to stop it. I started pushing him away. He kept saying; I don't have a choice. I begged him to tell the Marine Corps to send him to North Carolina. He kept saying I couldn't change my orders. I didn't want to hear him. I asked, why would you leave me? He left on orders, although he didn't want to leave. I felt abandoned and thought Calvin didn't fight hard enough for us to be together. I convinced myself he didn't care about the baby or me. I ended up writing to my oldest daughter's father about our daughter.

He started corresponding back and forth with me because I felt abandoned. I accepted his phone calls. I thought the Marine Corp would keep families together. I was naïve to the way things worked with the military. I was five months pregnant now. Late one night, I was having what I thought were Braxton hick contractions; the pain was unbearable. I rushed to the bathroom and saw blood and mucus in the toilet. I called out to my roommate Barb to take me to the hospital. I was losing the baby. So many pregnant Marines were miscarrying their babies, and I was next. When we arrived at the hospital, I was in labor, having contractions 10 minutes apart, and the doctor needed to stop my labor or lose my baby. I was stressed over Calvin leaving me. Barb was sitting in the room with me to keep me calm. The doctor prescribed this medication to stop the labor that made my body shake fast as if I had a seizure. I was scared because I couldn't make it stop. After several minutes, my body calmed down, and the contraction started slowing down until they stopped completely. The ultrasound revealed the sex of my baby, but I was so out of it that I didn't look at the monitor. I just wanted to go back to America. My first daughter's father, Brent, starts writing and calling me, saying once I get back to Georgia, I want to marry you. I will accept your baby as my child. I want to raise our daughter. I want to be in your life. I miss you. Just everything I needed to hear in my vulnerable state. I started thinking I needed to stay in the Marine Corp since I have a second child. Brent convinced me he had everything all together to take of the children and me, and after almost losing my baby twice, it was time to go. I started the process of leaving the Marine Corp. My Gunny was not happy with my decision. He kept saying, no, you're a good marine. Your sharp, you'll do well, you're going to go up the ranks. But no, I wanted to go back home to my high school sweetheart, not thinking about our issues, but his apology would erase the pain. I contacted Calvin and told him. I'm leaving. I'm getting out. I'm going back to Atlanta, and I'm getting married. I never knew how I devastated him. I was seven months pregnant when I processed out of the Marine Corps on January 29, 1990. I wasn't speaking to Calvin. My high school sweetheart is going to marry me. On February 14, 1990, we were married at the Dekalb County Courthouse with no rings. We never had a wedding or reception. He didn't have a house, only an apartment. He takes me to the apartment with only his bedroom furniture. The rest of the apartment was empty. I did not verify anything he was telling me before I decided to leave the Marine Corp. He was working at this warehouse job with guys who smoked weed and drank a lot. He started bringing people home from his job to hang out at the apartment. I did not know these guys, and I was afraid for my daughter. I knew what happened to me as a child. I didn't ask any questions about how he would take care of us. I was so mad at myself for my decision to leave the Marine Corp. After two weeks and eight months pregnant, I left my husband and moved in with my mom. I had to travel to Fort Gordon, GA, to give birth to my baby because the Marine Corp would only pay for it if I delivered on a military base. On March 18, 1990, my mom decided to take me to my grandmother's house in High Park, close to the hospital. On March 20, I started losing fluid, and my grandmother called my aunt to take me to the hospital. My best friends Winona and Denise checked on me throughout the day. I was in the room by myself, trying to watch TV and deal with the contractions. I refused all pain medication and an epidural because of my first experience with them. My contractions went from 5 minutes apart to 20 minutes apart. The doctor decided to break my water to speed up my contractions. It worked, but I was not dilating fast enough. In the room alone, back labor contraction, no water to cushion the contractions, no pain medication, and no Calvin. We had not spoken to each other after I decided to get married. It never crossed my mind he would not be at the birth of his child before he left Okinawa. I started throwing up and felt pushed by mistake. I could feel my baby's head coming out. I started screaming out to anyone. The baby is coming to Help me. Help me; the baby is coming. The nurse came in to check me and saw the head coming out. I was rushed to the delivery room, taking short breaths to keep from pushing again. They moved me from my bed onto the delivery table, and I pushed; it was a girl. She was born at 3:13 pm weighing 5.9 pounds Ashley Denise Burnett. I stayed in the hospital for four days before being discharged. I am back at my mother's house; I am 22 years old with two children, a four-year-old and a four-month-old. I had to find a job quickly, or she would make me get welfare. I was hired for a one-year assignment as a casual clerk at the main post office on Crown Road. I started the paperwork to get a divorce. I needed to make things right with Calvin. I never told him I had our baby or filed for divorce. I made the call, and he was happy to know his daughter was born but upset I waited so long. He wanted to come to Georgia to see her immediately. I told him it was fine. He told me he had a girlfriend and wanted to bring her. I had matured from my first daughter's situation. I told him that was fine too. I knew deep down inside he never tried to hurt me. I was the one who hurt him. The meeting went well, and he immediately started child support. He was upset my husband's name was on the birth certificate, and her last name was Nelson. He files all necessary papers to remove my husband's name, place his name on the birth certificate, change her last name to Burnett, and legitimize her. He added her information into the military system under his name. My divorce process was moving slowly. After the Desert Storm war started in 1991, I received military orders to return to active duty in North

Carolina. My lawyer used the military orders to expedite my divorce. My concern was whether I was legally married and if something had happened to me. The judge signed my divorce papers on my birthday September 6, 1990. I made everything suitable for my children and corrected all my wrongs with the fathers. He always did right by her. When his B. A. Q. increased with the military, he raised my child support. He made sure he paid for activities, bought her first car, or sent extra money. She didn't see him enough to build the father-daughter bond. He is currently married, and I get along with his wife. I was finally divorced. I'm out of the Marine Corps. I had to live off the money I saved from the Marine Corps. I started working at the U. S. Postal Service as a temporary employee. I was dating Matthew Price, who went to the same high school as my high school sweetheart. He told me he wanted to pursue me in high school, but I never noticed him. I have a dark complexion, and most dark complexion men did not date me. He was an attractive man. He looks like Michael Jordan. He favored Michael Jordan to the point one night, we were out at a local club, and people would scream, hey, Michael Jordan is in the house. Women were running over to him. He started laughing. No, I'm not Michael Jordan. We both worked at the post office as temporary employees. We were great friends and decided to take it to the level of a sexual relationship. We were not in a committed relationship, and he would go out with other women. I chose to only have sex with him. We looked out for each other. Matthew took me on a date one night because I worked so much. His mother offered a room for me to rent at her house. She was a kind and caring person. My girls and I moved in with her temporarily. I choose to become a police officer instead of a nurse. We applied for a position as a police officer with the Dekalb County Police Department. Department, as well. I was thinking I would be officer-friendly working in the school. Not the reality of working shifts, running after people, being shot at, fighting people, and dealing with a toxic work environment. I wasn't afraid to do the job, especially after my Marine Corp training mentally and physically. He made sure my girls and I didn't need anything. After almost a year of processing through the hiring stage of becoming a police officer, my job ended at the post office. I was currently working as a security guard at the Southern Company/Georgia Power office building. Our non-committed relationship faded into a non-sexual relationship. The office building was full of corporate America employees. Most of the employees were of upper-middle-class or upper-class status. They wore expensive clothes, perfume, cologne, and jewelry and drove high-end vehicles. Other security guards warned me that the employees were snobs and arrogant. They look down on us because we are security guards without a college degree or technically savvy. My interaction with the employees was all positive. My uniform was clean and neat, and my fantastic hairstylist, Debra Price, did my hair every week. I spoke proper corporate verbiage and carried myself with poise. Most of the employees were Caucasian. Daily the employees stopped by my security desk for a brief conversation. Some would say you speak very well; not sure what they expected of me. One IT tech trained me on their computer systems. He said I should go to college and work here because I learned so quickly. I should have listened to him. The black females were the last employees to speak to me. Finally, one black female complimented my hair and asked for my hairstylist's information. The females asked me to come to eat lunch with them regularly. Then it happened. I noticed a tall, dark, handsome black male going in and out of the building past my guard station. He was muscular and bowlegged. He asked for my phone number and a date. He started hanging out at my desk because we worked the same shift. I never did anything inappropriate at the job. After a few months, one of the females told me he was a married man. I confronted him, and he confirmed. Why do I keep attracting married men? The relationship ended. Southern Company signed a contract with a different security company, and I would not have a job. The new security company hired me. I met another guy who worked in the mailroom. He informed me he wanted to be a police officer too. He did not want to work in the mailroom forever. He took me out on a couple of dates. Before I left, we became friends, he stayed at Southern Company, and we would communicate here and there. On May 11, 1992, I started the police academy, and my friend Matthew rescheduled to begin in July. We had 21 recruits consisting of 19 males and two females. I was the only black female in my academy. However, the lead instructor in our class was a black female. The other female was transferred out of the academy to another job within the Dekalb County government. I was the only female, and some guys struggled to keep up with me. When they found out I was a Marine, they changed their idea of me and my abilities. A few guys took me under their wings to ensure I was strong enough on the streets. We started running and going to the gym. A few weeks one of the male instructors said, be careful, Crawford, because these men will be crazy over you and throughout the police department. Don't get your money and honey at the same place.

Chapter 3

After graduating from the police academy, my first assignment was at the South Precinct behind South Dekalb Mall. I had a thing about a man in a military or police uniform; they were disciplined. I was casually dating different people, not sexually involved. My focus was on learning how to police and survive on the streets. I saw this officer who caught my attention; it is better to say I caught his attention. His name was Darryl; he had a twin sister. He carried himself differently. How he wore his uniform, clean cut. His uniform was tailored meticulously, and his boots were shining. I realize Calvin was the same way about how they cared for themselves. Darryl has obsessive-compulsive disorder (OCD). We communicated over the police computer (KDT} because we worked together in the same territory. He did not socialize with many people at the job. Several officers said he was mean and arrogant. He was very nice and a jokester to my friends and me. Eventually, we started seeing each other outside of work. I can't tell you why I was head over heels for Darryl, but I was. I made the mistake of getting my honey and money in the same place. I knew he liked expensive things, and he spoiled himself. He didn't have children, and at that time, I had two girls. Nothing added up to a future with him because of my family dynamics when I think about it. He introduced me to a radio operator through the computer that covered our radio traffic on the shift at work. He said it was good to communicate with the radio operators. They are your lifeline out there. One operator I wrote was extremely funny with her jokes about life. We all talked back and forth on the police computer throughout my shift to make the day go by faster. At work, things began to change, moving to different shifts and territories. One night he called to see what territory I was working. He asked me to stop by during my shift. I agreed, and we continued to talk until I received a 911 call. After I handled the call, I headed toward his apartment. I made several calls on the way, but no answer. I knock on the door; he barely opens it. He was like, hey, I have company, which threw me off. Why did you ask me to come over here while on duty? He just apologized, and I walked away. My head started hurting so bad. It put me into a whirlwind, and I tried to keep it together at work. One of the veteran officers called me over the police radio and told me to meet with him. He said my voice did not sound right over the radio. Asking, are you okay? I told him what had transpired, do not worry, you will make it through. I discovered the radio operator he introduced me to be the girl at his house that night, and they have been dating for a year and a half. She and I began to compare notes. I didn't have anything against her. I don't know why he introduced her to me. I thought he liked to keep his women close, so he had control. Her name was Kathy. By the time we found out what Darryl was doing, we were cool friends. We had talked about visiting Washington D. C. to see the monument riding the Amtrak. I had never traveled on a train and wanted to experience it. After everything happened, we purchased train tickets, and off we went to Washington DC for a few days. He was playing both of us. She was his girlfriend for about a year when he started pursuing me. We enjoyed sightseeing and hanging out as tourists, not mentioning his name until the last day. Comparing all the actions he made with her and with me. We were able to connect as friends. I believe she confronted him when we got back in town because they were in a committed relationship. I confronted him about everything, and I made excuses because we did not commit to the relationship. He admitted to everything but said I should not be upset. We broke things off. She broke things off with him as well. He wrote me a long letter, apologizing and saying that he did wrong. I deserve better; I was a good person, he took me through some craziness, and we went our separate way. Years later, we connected again but only sexually. I knew it would not be anything more. I heard rumors that he told other officers I was off-limits, yet we were not in a relationship. This young officer named Carl Stilson did not care about the rumors and approached me. He is my third daughter's father, a Dekalb County police officer. I did not want Darryl to find out about him before telling him. I don't know why I was so concerned about hurting Darryl. Yet, in my mind, I would hurt him by dating another police officer at the same precinct. Police Officer relationships could get crazy, especially when told it's best not to date each other. We were in a dangerous environment. Yes, I told Darryl before it got out, and he was unhappy. Carl and I worked in the same territory and responded to 911 calls. We talked over the police computer at work, but nothing disrespectful and something that would have gotten us in trouble. We saw each other as far as I know; he wasn't dating anyone specifically in the department, but it wasn't a committed relationship. Once again, I am with a man who was meticulous about everything. His obsessive-compulsive disorder (O. C. D.) was worse than any men I had dated. They were all meticulous and immaculate and clean cut. But Carl was when I remember going over to his house; he would measure the distance between his remote controls, hangers, watches, jewelry, and shoes with a ruler. They were all covered in a line, just like in the military. I moved one to see if he noticed, and yes, he did. He was also in the Marine Corps. My first and second daughters' fathers were Marines, as well. We stopped seeing each other because he dealt with personal issues that affected his job. I later found out a young lady came after him for child support. He showed me a picture of the baby, and I told him to stop fighting her because the baby looked like him. While at the airport picking up my cousin Pam for my ten-year class reunion. I picked up the payphone when I heard this deep Barry White voice state; I wish I were on the phone talking to you. He said he was waiting on his flight to fly to New Jersey. With that New Jersey accent and the deep voice, I told him, you can give me your phone number. I called him a few days later because I wanted to hear his voice. Malik was an IT tech programming the Crown Plaza Ravinia computer system. He lives in New Jersey, but he was working on this project. He will be here for a year until he gets another assignment. Hanging out with him was amazing. He treated all my girlfriends like Queens. It was always a big group of us wining and dining. I traveled out of town with him, met several family members, and stayed at his apartment in New Jersey. When he was assigned to a work assignment in Germany and asked me to visit him. I wasn't feeling this long-distance situation and was concerned about how often I would see him. Carl reached out to me, wanting to get things started again. He apologized for disappearing and wanted to handle the situation. Malik asked me again to come to visit him in Germany. I thought this was an opportunity to use my passport and see my friend again. I was torn about my feelings for Malik and Carl. Carl got back into my ear, knowing I was flying to Germany. We liked each other, and that night my daughter was conceived. Four days later, I flew to Germany for ten days to visit Malik.

While in Germany, we talked, and things were over between us. Although I convinced myself before I left for Germany, I would not have sex with Malik; I did once in the ten days I was there. I missed my period and found out I was pregnant. I was honest with Carl about what happened, and he said it wasn't his child. Malik did not believe it was his child. I felt like a bitch for doing something like this to them. How do I prove it to Carl when I know the dates were very close? I wanted a paternity test, but Carl refused to get one. In my third pregnancy, I am alone with no help from either person. It is my fault, and I had to make things work. I told my girls, and they were excited about having a baby brother or sister. I was between living situations. I was homeless, working as a police officer, and pregnant. My mom moved to New Jersey and decided to sell her house. My little brother was the only one living there. My lease was up at my apartment, and I didn't have the security payment to get another apartment. I was on light duty and could not work a part-time job to make ends meet. My mom didn't want me to stay at her house because she wanted it to look like no one lived there. My mom didn't know I was pregnant. I would go to her house to take a shower, bathe, and feed my girls. I would sleep in my car in her driveway with my girls. We would go to the house in the morning to prepare for school and work. I went for several days not eating to have enough money to feed my girls. No one knew what I was going through because I kept a smile at work. A friend of mine from the Marine Corp contacted me to ask if I would be her roommate when she moved to Georgia. I quickly agreed, found a rental house, and put down the security and first month's rent. I loved the neighborhood and house. I purchased my first cellphone, and financially things were getting better. My pregnancy was stressful, and I lost fluid around my baby, assigned to bed rest. I would not have enough sick leave time to cover my six-week recovery. My contraction started on July 13 rushed to the hospital, but it was a false alarm. On July 15, the contractions started again 5 minutes apart, and they rushed to the hospital with a false alarm. On July 17 at 4 am, I was awakened with severe pain; I got up to go to the bathroom. I hear a loud pop and water gushing everywhere. I start screaming, waking up my girls, my roommate, and her five-year son. My water broke, and the baby is coming. We were running everywhere but to the car. The urge to throw up, but I couldn't because of my previous experiences. We make it to the hospital, and I sign in at 6 am. I was sent to labor and delivery and prepping for my doctor. I told the nurse I needed to throw up, and yes, it made me push. I couldn't control it, and the nurse told me she was ready. I pushed one time, and at 6:11 am, baby Crawford was here, weighing 7.3 pounds Aria Winona-Nicole Crawford. I couldn't decide on a name, so she was baby Crawford for two days. A coworker and her Godfather named her Aria. Her middle name came from my best friend, Winona Maolud and Nicole. I filed for child support against Carl, and he was ordered to take the test. I never lied to either one of them. They thought about how they thought about me, but I owned up to what I did. Not long after that, I found out Malik was legally married. I did not tell him how I found out, but it was through a relative of his, and when I confronted him, he responded legally separated. We weren't together, but on paper, you were legally married. Carl had already gone through a paternity battle with his other daughter's mother. I did not want to put more pressure on him. One of the discussions we used to have before we got involved was him denying being the father of another child. I had to prove that he was the father. His other daughter looked just like him; I was like, I don't know how you deny her. You are denying my daughter, who looks just like you. The paternity test read 99.9%, revealing he was the father. He wasn't paying child support. I asked him to pay for her childcare; that's what I need help with right now. I raised my other two daughters, eleven and seven years old. When my daughter was two and half years old, we went to court for child support. I had to bring my daughter to court with me. When we were in the lobby, he walked past us as if we did not exist. A lady sitting near me asked if your daughter's father because she looked like him. I answered, yes, she said that was cruel. I volunteered to go to court only to ensure I got everything for my daughter. The conversation just ended. We went through that process and had to return to court on a different day. He was not in child support court when I requested the same amount of money; he paid the first mother of his child. His lawyer was shocked by my request and thankful. When Carl returned to court, I watched his reaction when his lawyer informed him about my request, and he smiled. I just wanted him to be a part of my daughter's life. That was over, and we can move forward. Although I lived in Newton County, I received a phone call from Sergeant Little, with Dekalb County police, telling me not to leave the house. Something is going on with Carl and his fiancé. They were involved in a domestic dispute resulting in him physically attacking her. She sustained visible injuries. We don't know where he's at or something to that effect. I didn't know his address, but we lived close to each other. I received another phone call saying that he's barricaded himself up in his house. I turned on the television; it was not on the news. The police were trying to negotiate with him to get the children out. She immediately called back; he released the children. A sergeant demanded his Dekalb County badge and weapon from him. It was stated by several people on the scene that this was when he snapped by pulling out his gun and told everybody to "Get the Fuck" out of his house. He pointed his weapon, and everyone backed up and barricaded themselves in the house.

Sergeant Little called me again and asked whether I had a phone number for his best friend. They're negotiating with him to come out of his house. I gave her the phone number. I even tried to call his best friend, but he didn't answer the phone. I spend the entire day at home with my children. Before Carl and I stopped speaking to each other, we talked about officers losing their jobs, getting in trouble at work, and ending up on the news. Over our career, officers were committing suicide in unknown situations. Carl even joked about never killing himself because he loved himself too much. I was praying the hostage situation would not make the news; I didn't think he could handle the embarrassment in front of his coworkers. I started watching the news at 6 pm. The breaking news was about a domestic murder/suicide in Dekalb County, not related. Typically, anything dealing with a police officer would be breaking news. I felt a sense of relief because the evening news was about to go off. Maybe he surrendered and got the help he needed. At about 6:25 pm, the news anchor cuts the Newton County Sherriff Department is negotiating with a DeKalb County Police detective who has barricaded himself in his house. I couldn't breathe and prayed he was not looking at the news. Although we weren't speaking, I remembered our good conversations and never doing something to embarrass himself. Around 10 pm or so, I needed to go to the grocery store. I called Sgt Little to see if she had an update because I needed to leave the house to go to the grocery store. She informed me that he had stopped answering the phone, and they were waiting on the response of the Dekalb County Fire Department to make force entry. As I was driving back home from the store, I noticed a Dekalb County Fire Truck pass me, heading in the direction of Carl's house. I received a phone call from Lieutenant Ann Willis about thirty minutes later. She said they made entry, and he committed suicide. Self-inflicted gunshot to his head. I started crying so bad, but she stayed on the phone until I calmed down. They argued about the child support papers and how many more women will prove you are the father of their baby. He was dealing with abandonment issues because his biological parents gave him up. People were making jokes at work about the situations. Some people blamed me, and others said I did the right thing asking for child support. I didn't go to his funeral. I had to get myself together. He fought a battle no one knew about, and losing his job was the final straw. After a few months, his sister decided to talk to me. All the rumors she heard about me were false. Carl and I had a great friendship before all of this happened. He was upset with me for going to the child support people; we did not have any issues. Eventually, his best friend, Steve, contacted me. He said the day Carl took his life, he accidentally left his phone at home. Steve spoke with Carl's adopted father about my daughter Aria. His adopted parents were Swedish, and Carl spent seven years living abroad. He acknowledged he had another daughter but hadn't given them enough details to contact me. They wanted to be a part of her life. Aria and her siblings would spend time together at their grandparents' house. Every December 16, they celebrated their dad's birthday by visiting him at the mausoleum. It still plays in my head about him taking his life. His adopted mother passed away a couple of years later from breast cancer. I was on my own with three daughters. Calvin helped as much as possible, and Carl's survivor benefits helped with Aria's daycare bill. I knew it was time to purchase a home because I was tired of moving every year. I worked part-time jobs to pay off debt and clear my credit. I was working at Publix three to four days a week. I met a guy named Theolos, who I called Theo. He was training for the Assistant Manager in position in the produce department. He was in his 15th year with the company. He was very friendly and had a good conversation. He surprised me with a dozen of roses one night at work. He wanted to introduce me to his mom and only sister within weeks of meeting him. He had a two-year son that he took care of in Florida. I thought it might be moving quickly. He assured me he liked me. I told him I had three daughters and did not have time for games. I continued to judge myself for having three children. What do other people possibly think of me? My self-image was low. I met his mom and sister. He met my daughters, and things were going great. Five months later, I was pregnant again. Theo proposed to me at his mom's house. I was ready to get married. Working as a police officer with three daughters was hard enough, mainly because of shift work and part-time jobs. He prepped for the assistant manager and then manager in less than a year. He started working at Publix at the age of 15. I saw stability and longevity. Although I respected him, I was not in love with him. We moved forward in our relationship and raised my daughters. Our wedding day was August 25, 1998. I was open and honest with the pastor about my past during marriage counseling; however, my fiancé was dishonest and judged me. Our pastor told us not to get married based on his analysis. His grandmother, whom he loved dearly, passed away on August 25. We decided to move forward with the relationship for the children's sake. We did not want our child born out of wedlock, so on November 21, 1998, I went against the recommendation of the marriage counselor and married Theo. We moved into a rent-free apartment as they completed our new house. My girls were happy, and I thought things were going great. Then, after 15 years, he suddenly quits his job without talking it over with me. How could you quit your job? We just got married. Our son was due in January. I can't remember the exact day he quit his job. He took a lump sum of money from his stocks in the company. He went shopping, buying new clothes and sneakers. I was so upset with him, but what could I do. He said he wanted to be a private investigator. I didn't think he had the skill set to be a private investigator: he had no previous training or job knowledge. Things went downhill in our marriage quickly. On Sunday morning, January 3, I used the bathroom, but something was different; it was slimy fluid when I wiped. It smelled sweet like candy. I was thinking, did my water break. I told Theo what was going on and then called my doctor, who instructed me to go. Once, I was at the hospital, and a test confirmed that I was losing amniotic fluid. Unlike my previous births, I was relaxed, calm, and controlled. My doctor checked me once and told everyone to call her once I started throwing up. That was my signal that the baby was coming. I started throwing up like clockwork, and he was ready to be delivered. I took several pushes to the point I told the doctor he wouldn't come out. I was repositioned several times and exhausted from pushing with every contraction. I wanted to fight Theo for putting this big baby inside of me. The doctor had to refocus me. She calmed me down and said, you can do this. One long hard push, and I heard him crying. My son was born at 10:18 pm weighing 8.3 pounds Cortlan Savon Abrams.

When the apartment management company hired a new female leasing manager, she knew my limited duties as the apartment security police officer. My son was twelve days old. She asked about female officers' abilities to patrol the complex and protect the residents. I explained to her we had over seven years of law enforcement experience in the roughest part of DeKalb County. After leaving the meeting, a leasing agent informed us that the leasing manager wanted to replace us with male officers. A few days later, All-female officers received termination letters and three days to vacate the property or start paying rent. The stress was overwhelming then; my infant son started running a fever of 103 degrees. We rushed him to the hospital. My husband left me at the hospital with no food. I was at a children's hospital, which meant they were not responsible for feeding the parents. The nurse gave me juice and crackers. Unknown what caused his body temperature to spike, it returned to normal in three days. Returning to the apartment complex, preparing to move, my husband decided to quit his job. After about 30 days, I decided enough was enough. With his termination from his employment as a private investigator, he wasn't looking for another job because he wanted to be a record producer. He was lying around the apartment feeling sorry for himself. May 1999, I told him I wanted a divorce and gave back my ring. I did not wish to purchase the house and terminated the contract. I filed for divorce and then started looking for my own home. The other female officer and I filed an Equal Employment Opportunity Commission

EEOC complaint against the management company. We won the wrongful termination lawsuit for discrimination.

In July 1999, I purchased a four-bedroom house, and on the day of closing, I slept on the floor of my empty house. I was so proud of myself for giving my children a backyard. I went from homeless to living apartment rent-free to now a homeowner. I was working so much that I did not have time or want to date anyone. Denise wanted me to date a nice guy. She talked about her husband's best friend, Mason; we initially met in 1992 at our best friends' wedding. I was upfront with him about my situation. As we got to know each other, I felt he held back some vital information. I asked him, are you legally divorced? He finally admitted that we're not legally divorced. We're going through the divorce but have separated for over two years. My best friend thought the divorce was final, or she would have never suggested we get to know each other. By that time, we were living together, and he was helping me with the bills. Mason built a fantastic relationship with my son and told people that he was his child. I told my ex-husband, I've moved on; you can see your son; it's up to you. I kept the lines of communication open for Theo to be involved in his son's life. My relationship with Mason started getting weird because he received some mail from an unknown female.

He became secretive about his whereabouts and received strange phone calls late. I reached out to my best friend about my concerns. Her husband said he would reach out to his estranged wife because things were not adding up to him either. My best friend Denise called to tell me she was pregnant. Her husband was so excited to have a boy he sent a text message to Mason. Since he didn't respond to the text message, he called Mason, who hung up in his face. When Mason came home later that day, I asked if he got the great news about our best friend having a boy. He responded yes with an attitude and walked away from me. He was upset and jealous because he wanted a son. I told Mason I didn't want any more children. Things were not the same anymore, and he started experiencing health issues. The doctor instructed him not to go outside in the heat. Then, he would go outside in the middle of the day, the hottest part, and mow the lawn. He would come in the house shaking as if he was about to pass out. I called Denise to ask if Mason had had a stroke. She replied no however he did have a TIA or a mini stroke. I asked him why he would put himself in harm's way. No answer from him. One day a lady came banging on my door screaming, your husband needs help. I didn't know who she was talking about because I was not married. I ran outside to find Mason lying on the ground, slightly under my car shaking. I called 911, but he kept screaming, don't call 911. He was transported and released later the same day. I couldn't take any more of the lies or half-truths. I reached out to my best friend and her husband. I told them everything I was observing with Mason and how it stressed me out. He was legally married, and I had no say over his treatment if something happened to him. They reached out to his wife, and she agreed to meet with my best friend's husband. She wanted to talk with me directly which I agreed. We talked for about two hours or so. Our stories were identical, and I was willing to testify at her custody hearing. He informed me that he had to have surgery, and afterward, I drove him to his parents' house to recover. I went back to my house and packed all his belongings. He picked up his belongings and then started calling my cellphone and house phone, begging me to take him back. I received over 45 phones over two days. If he made one more phone call, I obtained a warrant for harassing phone calls. The phone calls stopped. The story behind my youngest daughter's father has a lot of turns and twists. Let's go back to the airport and the guy with the deep Barry White voice. Well, Malik and Gabe are cousins. I dated Malik, who lived out of town, and later found out he was married. Then I got pregnant close to when I dated Carl. I visited Malik in New Jersey at what I thought was his apartment but found out it was Gabe's apartment. When my third daughter was born, Gabe was very concerned about me. He saw a picture of Aria and quickly said it was Malik's child based on her nose. Gabe always talked about his dissatisfaction with the size of the family nose. He would pay for a nose job if he ever had a child. I knew it was a possibility but felt that Carl's daughter was deep in my heart. Gabe occasionally stayed in contact with me to see how I was doing and talked about life. I decided to introduce him to a childhood girlfriend to make a love connection. He spoke positive things about the relationship. Gabe moved from New Jersey and purchased a house in Georgia. Gabe was nine years older and worked in corporate America in a management position. Financially Gabe did very well for himself. He enjoyed living in Georgia, working at his company, and the simple life. One day I received a phone from Gabe to visit him at his home and hang out. We went to a local restaurant, talked about relationships and work-related things, and had a few drinks. I talked to him on my long drive back to my house. He told me things did not work out with my friend. He wanted to get to know me better. I questioned him about his cousin Malik. He tells me that Malik was married the entire time. He would bring women to his apartment as if it was his apartment. He had a wife and two small children. He thought I was cute the day he met me in New Jersey. I was not dating anyone, and Gabe was single as far as I knew. The Malik situation happened in 1996, and it is 2001 now. My mindset was I didn't care anymore. Gabe crossed the line by pursuing his cousin's ex. Malik was not forthcoming about his marriage, and I was wrong to be involved with both. I did not tell Malik I started dating his cousin. We began to hang out, go to dinner, watch movies, and get to know each other better. Not sure what day after the horrific incident on 9/11, he was laid off and received his servant pay. I went to the doctor for an unrelated issue. The doctor had to administer a pregnancy test before prescribing any medicine. I assured my doctor I was not pregnant. I was in the lobby of the doctor's office waiting for my prescription when the nurse called me back again. My doctor was sitting in the room waiting on me. He had a smirk on his face. You need to make an appointment with an OB/GYN doctor because you are pregnant. I laughed so hard. You almost had me, doc. I know I am not pregnant. He started laughing and said Ms. Crawford, I am telling the truth. I stared him down, waiting for him to say it was a joke, but he held his word. I was in disbelief and requested an ultrasound. The doctor had blood drawn, and the nurse did the ultrasound. I called Gabe with the news. His doctor said he could not have children, but I guess he did know about me. People are going to think I am the grandfather instead of the father. However, Gabe broke the pregnancy news to Malik. Malik called me and expressed his hurt, and I told him my feelings. I cared for Malik, but I knew I hurt him twice. I justified my actions in my head; you should have never pursued me in the first place. Of course, Gabe was doubtful of the paternity and my previous situation with his cousin Malik. We stopped speaking when I told him I was not having an abortion. I was taking care of my three girls and one son on my own. At this time, I had a 16-year-old, 12-year-old, 5-year-old, and 3-year-old. Near the end of my pregnancy, he called to check on me and find out the sex of our child. He was hoping for a boy since he was the only child. Well, it's a girl. I woke up at 4 am to prepare for work when I heard a loud pop. Oh no, my water broke. I don't think I thought this situation out. Samantha lived thirty minutes away from me, and the hospital was an hour away. Samantha was a police officer, and she drove like one that morning. I made it to the hospital in record time. I was prepped and ready to deliver, but my contraction slowed down. My little sister continued to call Gabe, but no answer. About 10 am, I received a phone call from him complaining my little sister left him a nasty message calling him all kinds of names. I did not care at that moment to hear anything. The contractions were 5 minutes apart. I was not dilated enough, and she needed to drop down some more. Since my first birth, I elected to have all-natural deliveries. I was taking the contractions like a trooper. Gabe decided to come and witness the birth of his only child. The contraction was two minutes apart, and Samantha stepped in to help me breathe through the contractions. When I started throwing up, I told them to call my doctor to come into the room and deliver my baby. I was ready to fight everyone's insight if they didn't get the baby out of me. Gabe was standing far enough away; I couldn't grab him. He was taking photos the entire time. At 11:51 am, she weighed 7.2 pounds, Gia Elize Mitchell. I allowed Gabe to name her because he was an only child and wanted her to have his initials.

Chapter 4

On January 29, I was officially honorably discharged from the United States Marine Corps, eight months pregnant and jobless. I was stressed out because my money was running low. After having difficulty finding a job, I went to the welfare office and completed the application. The welfare representative told me that my welfare check would start if I didn't contact her in ten days with a job. This information pushed me even harder to find employment. Finally, I was hired as a temporary, casual clerk at the post office on day seven. For my next task, I needed a vehicle. A friend of mine from the Marine Corps was selling his car for $2,000 cash. I was determined not to ask anybody for the money and worked as much overtime as possible. Working the night shift, I could not afford a babysitter during the day. I was nursing my baby, struggling to get sleep, and losing weight. People at my job were concerned about my weight loss because I dropped from 175 pounds to 120 pounds in four months. I collapsed at work because I was working too much, and my body finally shut down on me. The doctor said I was anemic and exhausted, and I knew I had to slow down. I bought my first car, a Volkswagen Rabbit. The atmosphere was toxic at the post office, like a soap opera show. Married employees swap partners and smoke weed or drink alcohol during their breaks. I had an older guy tell me

I had to go out with him, and when I refused, he followed me around, making crazy comments. He became very aggressive because I would not accept his advances, and he called me stuck up. I notified the postal police officers of my concerns. A few days later, someone punctured the side of three of my tires. I had to replace all of them. I went back to the postal police to explain I was in fear of my life. Two days later, it happened again, with three tires punctured the same way. I felt helpless, resigned, and started working as a security guard with Wells Fargo at Southern Company. I wanted a job to help prep me for becoming a police officer. The world was dealing with the Rodney King situation in California, and all police officers faced backlash. The hiring psychiatrist expressed I was very demanding of myself. I wanted to be as perfect as possible. Even though I took breaks between relationships, I still think I moved too fast. The psychological tests continued to show I was too demanding of myself. It didn't change. I excelled in the academy and was ready to hit the streets with my Field Training Officer (FTO). The South Precinct, the roughest area in Dekalb County, and my first choice. My first 911 call was an alarm call at a private school. While we searched the building for a possible burglar, a person walked past the door, and it freaked me out. My FTO laughed at me and then said it would be okay. I need to remember my military and police training, get my thoughts together and move forward.

I completed my eight-week FTO training. Foot chases were my favorite for two reasons. First, I caught people who ran from me. Secondly, the foot chases were safer than car chases that put other people in harm's way. My first supervisor was a white male, Sgt Howell, unit number 312, who did not show favoritism. He expected the officers to do their job, whether black or white. I was blessed to have him as one of my supervisors when I hit the streets. I paid attention to how he addressed our predominately black community. The police department needs more white supervisors like him to deal with diverse issues within the agencies. Around my six-month mark with the police department, I received a phone call from a male lieutenant on my off day. I thought he was calling about a schedule change. Instead, he talked about sexual things he wanted me to do to him. His voice slurred. I kept saying, sir, you have the wrong number. I realized he was on duty and drunk. I knew I did not deserve someone to act in this behavior towards me. I was so shocked and afraid to tell my supervisor because I was a rookie in the department, and they would blackball me for snitching. I trusted one officer and called to explain what had happened. He asked me If I was okay and stated he would handle it. I have no idea what he said or did, but the lieutenant apologized for his actions. Unfortunately, another female officer experienced a similar incident with the same lieutenant a few weeks later. I contacted the same officer, and again he apologized to her. My biggest concern was that this lieutenant behaved on duty and was intoxicated driving a police vehicle. Later in my career, I discovered that several supervisors were intoxicated by camouflaging their alcohol in coffee. I needed two years of patrol experience before applying for a specialized position. Black female officers worked undercover in prostitution, drug rings, dealing with underage alcohol, or something of that nature. I applied for as many training classes as possible because I believed an educated officer better serves the community. In addition, knowledge of the department's policies and procedures is necessary. I will go into more detail later in this chapter. My nickname was Policy Polly. I began to work part-time jobs to make ends meet. Eight hours on the job, dropping my children off to the babysitter, then putting in another four to eight hours at a part-time job throughout the night. I drank power drinks to stay awake and ate free food at different restaurants. My health was declining, and my weight was increasing. I started having heart palpitation, which I guessed from lack of sleep. I love the evening watch shift because of all the action—the most armed robberies, foot chases, shootouts, fights, etc. I could never imagine being threatened by my coworkers, but it happened. I do not remember what year this was in my career; however, it was early. A veteran police officer came to me and asked if I had made someone angry.

His question confused me; he handed me pink paper with my name on the top. He said someone placed it in his message box. The message read, "leave morning watch or else." He asked Crawford who would threaten you and why. This threat is serious for a police officer who is supposed to have your back. I didn't know who to trust because several months had passed, and there was no investigation. The new supervisor discovered my complaint hidden away in a file drawer. A fellow police officer has threatened me, and no one cares. On August 22, 1996, I had knee surgery to repair an ACL tear which placed me on light duty. During that week, I cleared, mailed, and organized the Sheriff's department's and Recorder's court warrants for the Warrant Officer. Upon his return, he wrote an excellent letter to my supervisor praising my work. The precinct commander approached me about an administrative officer's position. The position was 9 am to 5 pm, Monday through Friday, holiday and weekend off, and plainclothes. The decision changed the direction of my career in law enforcement. My work ethic has paid off. No one can say I slept my way to this position. I established excellent working relationships with other divisions and departments throughout the county, such as the Chief's Office, Human Resources, Solicitor's Office, District Attorney Office, Magistrate Court, DUI Court, Civil Court, and Recorder's, State Court, Training Division and Superior Court. I was the liaison to the community by receiving gratitude calls, complaint calls, setting up training dates, and much more. My position was very demanding and filled with deadlines which I consistently met on behalf of the Precinct Commander. From 1992- to 2005, I worked as a patrol officer, an undercover officer, administrative officer, crime analysis officer, fraud/general theft detective, and Homeland Security detective. I was offered a position with the Homeland Security division of Dekalb County as an administrative detective for Chief Eddison. The department was going through management changes with a new chief and administration. The Chief was not happy and rumored then held up the promotions, which affected my chance of becoming a sergeant from the current list. I was number twelve to be promoted from the list. The sergeant promotional list expired, and I had to wait and take the test a third time. Because the previous list expired, the administration immediately promoted eighteen new sergeants from the new list. I was tired of the games at Dekalb County Police Department. I applied for a position as an officer with the Marta Police Department. I excelled through the hiring process with Marta Police Department and was offered a job. I received a phone call informing me of my sergeant promotion the next day. I chose to stay at Dekalb County and accept my promotion. A lieutenant physically assaulted me. I was helping a sergeant because he needed a report on some crime stats located in my office. We were walking out of the roll call room towards my office. I assumed the lieutenant and another sergeant were heading to the captain's office. Instead, they walked into my office. As I continued to walk into my office, he turned, struck me in my chest, and pushed me back. He looked at me, slammed my door in my face, and locked it. Both sergeants and the administrative assistant witnessed the assault. I had on my bulletproof vest. I went into the women's bathroom and waited for the captain to return. I told the captain what happened, and he asked, do you want to make a formal complaint? Based on what had happened to me prior, I told him no; however, I would document the incident. I will destroy his career; they will hate me. The captain spoke to the lieutenant about putting his hands on me. He told the captain; that he didn't remember the incident, and the captain told him we had three witnesses. I did not want to be in the room with this lieutenant. About six years later, I was about to be promoted to lieutenant. I called a meeting with this lieutenant to discuss the incident. He says, I thought we were cool. I said, not cool enough for you to put your hands on me. He finally apologizes, and that is the end of it. In 2012, I was promoted and assigned to Center Precinct. Eight months later, I switched with another lieutenant and moved back to South Precinct. My position changed to an administrative lieutenant. I hated to leave my morning watch team because of the cohesiveness we built, and everything was working smoothly. I was honored that my work ethic paid off again. One thing guaranteed with the police departments is change. I moved to the narcotics unit. My work life was great, but my personal life was falling apart with my fiancé. We were attending premarital counseling for his infidelity. I was learning about my new position and the detectives working with me. I had to assume a new identity and stay a police officer simultaneously. I have been assigned an undercover take-home vehicle with a gas card, my own office, and more. The combination of this new position and the ups and downs in my personal life was the end of my police career with Dekalb County. It started with the undercover vehicle I chose to drive and its emission problem. Most undercover cars had mechanical issues from sitting so long in a warehouse. I went from a red 300Z to a beige Navigator to finally deciding on a white BWM 525i. It had a paper tag until the vehicle passed emission. I was given instructions to only fill up with premium gas using the purchase card or damage the engine. I took the BMW to the maintenance garage to complete an emission test. He instructed me to fill it up with premium gas, drive it on the highway for 100 miles, and return it. I contacted my captain to update him on the status of the emission test. I continued to drive the vehicle back and forth to work with only the paper tag. My daughter was involved in a car accident and needed to borrow my vehicle for a few weeks. I drove back and forth to work and stopped for groceries or gas in the BMW. The Rockdale County sheriff conducted a traffic stop about my paper tag. I explained the situation and my credential with the Dekalb County police department to the officer. I informed my captain about the traffic stop. I took the BMW to the maintenance garage for another emission test, and it failed again. I am working on my relationship with my fiancé. He wanted to start looking for our house to purchase together in Macon, GA. The maintenance person advised me to put highway miles on the vehicle to help it the emission test. I relayed this information to my captain. He stated the same thing happened to his daughter's car during the conversation. He told me to put premium gas in the car and drive it on the highway. I asked my captain if it was okay to drive it to Macon, GA, because I leave to come to work sometimes. He verbally approved one of the detectives currently working on a case in Macon, GA, and me. I failed to get this approval in writing. I was stopped a second time by another Rockdale County sheriff about the paper tag. Although I showed my credentials and explained the situation, this officer tried to give me a hard time about everything. After my daughter returned my vehicle, I drove my car to Macon. However, the captain verbally approves of responding to the BWM from Macon. I took the BWM for another emission test one afternoon before grabbing my lunch, and the vehicle failed. I was frustrated about the emission issues and tired of getting pulled over by the police. I called the captain because I remember having a conversation with him prior. I told him it still did not pass, and I was hungry. The maintenance person told me to drive it on the highway and bring it back this afternoon. I asked him if it was okay to drive it to Macon. I would grab my lunch and return to get the emission test. I notified my sergeants and the other lieutenant to cover me while getting this vehicle to pass the emission test. I gassed up the vehicle in Macon because the gas prices were lower than in the Atlanta area. Each time I put gas in the BMW, I printed the gas receipts and logged my name, badge number, and mileage. I turned all gas receipts in for accountability. During this time, I received a call from a retired Dekalb County police officer about an unrelated issue. She talked about needing to borrow a car for two weeks because she was involved in an accident. I told her it was okay to use my vehicle because the captain approved me to drive the BMW to and from Macon on occasions. Other than that, I drove the BMW straight home after work. I asked for another vehicle and requested to take the BMW to the dealership for maintenance. The news stations and newspaper outlets covered stories about the misuse of the purchase card by Dekalb County government officials. They were making purchases for their homes, vacations, and other personal items. The police department elected to do an internal audit of any purchases made in all divisions. I enjoyed the cohesiveness of the team. Working Narcotics is a dangerous job, and your mind must be clear. In December 2014, I validated that my fiancé had cheated and engaged to another woman. Six months later, this woman is dead of a gunshot to the head in his bedroom. I will go into more detail later in the book. I am a police officer and did not want to be mixed up in this mess and needed to protect the county. I wasn't sleeping and thought of not wanting to be here anymore. I made an appointment with Kaiser Permanente Behavior Health to speak with a therapist. I was diagnosed with major depression and placed on FLMA for six weeks. I was required to attend a mandatory group session with ten other people three times a week. I was released to full duty and quickly placed on administrative leave pending an Internal Affairs investigation about my gas purchases in Macon, GA. I didn't think anything because the captain approved me, purchased the cheapest gas, signed, and turned in my receipts weekly. I had nothing to hide and did everything per policy. My captain denied ever giving me verbal approval. It was a downward spiral from this point on. I could not locate the emails and text messages between my captain and me during the investigations. My assumptions are they took my county phone, and I assume, erased the text messages, and disabled my email with the conversations. I was allowed to resign instead of termination. I accepted that it was my fault and my choice to drive to Macon, GA I walked away from the only source of income. I found a job at a security company for three months. I lost my house, my vehicle, and almost my life. I was embarrassed for my children and family. I filed for bankruptcy and applied for food stamps and Medicaid. I was in college full time and lived off my refund check, my separation money from Dekalb County, and my income tax check until I found another job. A local college police department hired me for the first Captain position. After leaving the county, I found the photo evidence sent to the captain. The supervisor knew my whereabouts because he responded to my text message photos; he was clear about everything. I am at peace; I knew the truth, and so does God.

Chapter 5

After leaving Dekalb County negatively, my post certification as a police officer was pending a Georgia Peace Officer Standards and Training Council (P.O.S.T.) investigation. I submitted my rebuttal letter to the investigator as instructed in my paperwork. My last official day at Dekalb County was September 2, 2015. On September 7, 2015, my new job was Lieutenant/Operations Commander at a security company. I worked together with an amazing young lady named Sonya Hollowell. The income would not sustain my children and me. The company did not pay the officers very well, which caused a high turnover rate. One day Chief Eddison told me to check the status of my POST certification. He knew I missed law enforcement and wasn't happy at my current job. I didn't want to see it; I was embarrassed. I checked for status, which read, you may hire; this meant any police agency could hire me as a police officer at any rank I qualified. I applied at several agencies at the campus police departments to surround myself with educators and college students. I dreamed of teaching at a campus college. I contacted the POST investigator; she did not see anything to stop me from applying. I applied to the Atlanta Metropolitan State College Department of Public Safety for a police officer position. I had to do it for my children and set my pride aside. As I was going through the hiring process, a captain position came available. I declined the police officer position and applied. The interview process was challenging. A panel of four ranking people asked me twenty situational questions. I got the job. On April 2, 2016, the first day of work started with an incident that gave me a clear vision of how campus and traditional policing differed. It was a smaller agency of twenty-one employees. Dekalb County had over 800 plus employees. At one point, I supervised over thirty officers. I had to learn how to scale it down when dealing with students and faculty personnel. I felt like I was back in the political era of policing again. My chief never worked at a traditional police department. However, he had the skillset to do his job. I was very open and honest throughout my whole process about what had transpired in my personal life. I didn't want him blindsided because the case was still pending. Was it a suicide as reported by my ex-fiancé or a murder? People make mistakes every day. Just don't lie about it. With integrity, you can recover from any situation eventually. I quickly realized I had walked into a live beehive at the agency. The rumor around the department was the female lieutenant wanted the captain's position. I was the first captain of the department, and she resented me for this. I only wanted to focus on doing my job and helping with the department's operation. Instead, I was dealing with a black female ranking officer who hated the sight of me. I thought I would never have ever seen someone who hated me so much in my life. Just because in her eyes, I took her position. There is no proof of who, but someone submitted a complaint stating the department hired a security officer arrested for murder. The allegation was severe. The internal auditor, chief, and I had an emergency meeting. I had to reveal to another person my situation to assure the auditor it was a false allegation directed at me. No one could understand the stress and anxiety I was dealing with because I believed my ex-fiancé. When she bought up the murder arrest, it opened wounds that did not belong at my job. Things got progressively worst with this female, and I felt as if my hands were tied. Next, the POST mandate office received a letter accusing me of being involved in two murders. That was a lie. The internal auditor stated she had not received these many complaints from our department until April 2016. I had severe headaches, which I did not tell anyone. I sat in my office for several days and cried to relieve myself from the pain. I had to file for bankruptcy which meant I was losing my house. I was in college full-time, maintaining an A average. I graduated magna cum laude. Yet I had to go to work under all this stress and run the operations of the police department. Things progressed slowly, and the department experienced a lot of turnovers for better pay at a more central agency. I received notification from POST counsel that my investigation was final with No Action/Agency actions. It was finally over, and I could go on with my law enforcement career. They expected me to operate in a chief compacity; without giving me the title. I asked why he hadn't sat down to counsel me if I was doing poorly and not qualified. He could not say anything negative or what I needed to improve. He left my office and later texted me to look at my POST certification history. I am Acting Chief of Atlanta Metropolitan State College. I sent in my request for additional temporary pay and was approved. I was tired of allowing people to walk over me. I worked a lot and never got compensated. I usually would not have stepped up and requested more money. I would have just accepted and continued to do my job. It was time for growth, to stand up for myself and get what I deserved. After hiring the new chief, I stepped down from a captain's position and took an officer position at another college. My experience at the new college was not favorable. I received an email to report to the auditor's office. Within weeks of starting my new job, someone made an anonymous complaint about favoritism through the University System of Georgia complaint line. It is happening again. The pandemic hit the world, and everything shut down. As police officers, we needed to change our approach to policing during this time for safety. Some officers refused to clean up after themselves, including not wearing masks. I continued to get sick and ended up in the emergency room. At the beginning of 2020, I joined a network marketing company called Total Life Changes. I watched a friend on social media talk about her journey with detoxing daily, drinking a liquid multivitamin, losing weight, and getting energy from a pill called N.R.G. It worked. I lost forty pounds, and the skin on my face cleared up. I was so excited, but I didn't have to tell anyone. Instead, the phone started ringing, and my direct message on social media filled up with questions. What are you doing to look like that? Although my physical part was changing, my mental part moved slowly. I attended therapy sessions to deal with the stress from the job and my personal life. I started meditating with the group in October 2020 and listened to two coaching calls a month. I had never spoken affirmations over myself before joining this group. It changed my perspective of myself. I deserved more, and I was going to get it. I made sure leaving the police department and the college would not affect my master's degree. I spoke with my chief about retiring from law enforcement altogether. He gave me his blessings and thanked me for the services. Most of my law enforcement career satisfied life lessons, and I met many beautiful citizens and coworkers throughout my career. I have been able to mentor new officers. The most important lesson learned is if it's not in writing means not approved. The biggest takeaway is don't lie about anything because that allows you to recover and keep your integrity. On February 12, 2021, I retired from law enforcement. On May 15, 2021, I graduated with my master's degree. I am doing Total Life Changes on a full-time basis. I have partnered with my sponsor Dedra Smith and worked with Winona Wills to create Mind, Body & Beyond with one of my best friends. My life continues to evolve to a better me.

Chapter 6

I was introduced to William by a coworker at Dekalb County. She was also in the National Guard Air Force with him. August 2005, Michelle, and I were riding in the detective vehicle, following up on some cases. She asked if I was dating anyone at the time because she wanted to introduce me to this fine man from her military unit. She kept saying he was fine and intelligent with hazel eyes. I laughed because I always attracted guys with hazel, green or blue eyes. She said we would look so good together. Michelle decided to call William at his job, although I pleaded with her not to do it. He answered the phone, and Michelle told him she wanted him to speak with me and put the phone up to my ear. I rolled my eyes at Michelle for putting me on the spot. We spoke briefly and exchanged phone numbers and work email addresses. I was flying out to Las Vegas to celebrate my 38th birthday in a few weeks. I explained I was not ready to meet anyone new in my life. I didn't need a man making a judgment on me. He started calling me regularly with great conversation. He would send nice text messages and ask me about the day. We decided to send a photo of ourselves since we had not met. He lived in Macon, GA, an hour away from me. He sent a photo of himself in his Air Force honor guard uniform to my work email. We all circled my computer to analyze his photo. It was official William fine. He told me he loves chocolate women after he saw my photo. After several conversations about our childhood, family, and careers, we planned to meet in person. I decided to inform him I was a mother of five children and had divorced twice. He told me he was a father of three children and divorced once. We continue daily phone conversations. My coworker Angela and I had a training class in Forsyth, GA, which was twenty-five minutes from his house. Angela and I decided to get a hotel room and go down to Forsyth the night before. Our training class started at 0800 am we did not want to rush in the morning. William came to the hotel to meet me for the first time because we spent weeks and hours talking on the phone. Michelle spoke highly of him, so I felt comfortable meeting him in person. He was a big Atlanta Falcon fan, and they played the Philadelphia Eagles that night. He headed to the hotel during halftime to meet me. I heard the knock on the door. I looked through the peephole. I was like a kid in a candy store and ran across the room before opening the door. He was looking and smelling good. We all watched the game, and the Falcons won. He decided to book a hotel room instead of driving back to Macon. He asked me to come by his room before I went to sleep. I was nervous, but I knew how to fight, and Angela knew how he looked. We talked for a while, but I had an early morning class. I was heading back to my room when he said I was welcome to stay with him. Nothing will happen; just sleep. I told Angela I would see her in the morning. We were in bed, fully dressed. He moved closer, whispering, let's spoon. We decided to take it farther, and I asked him if he had protection. His answer was yes, and he pulled a gun out of his bookbag. I held my breath because it caught me off guard. I had my gun, but it wasn't within my reach. He started laughing and said, you asked if I had protection. I exhaled and said a condom, silly. Yes, I have one. The attraction was strong between us, and we had sex that night. The next morning, he took my suitcase to my car, kissed me, and told me to have a great day. He sent me wonderful text messages throughout the day. We talked on the phone daily; he invited me to Macon to hang out. He decides to get a hotel room again. I was not coming down again if I could not come to his house. On my next visit to Macon, I went to his clean and neat townhouse. After that visit, William stopped calling me. I made several calls with no answer. I assumed he had disappeared because the holidays were approaching. I started working twelve to sixteen-hour days preparing for the holidays and keeping my mind drama-free. I did not know what had happened to him. We did not speak to each other for about two months before he called; I ignored his calls for a week. I finally answered the phone, and he kept apologizing for disappearing. He explained he needed time to deal with his situation but no details. He wanted to see me again; I said yes. He asked me to come to dinner with him in Macon. I met him at the restaurant, but I wasn't expecting to meet his father, mother, two sisters, and nieces. I was not mentally ready for this and was extremely nervous. I whispered to him, why didn't you tell me I was meeting your family. He smiled and didn't respond. We sat down, and I felt his sisters were staring at me but not in a positive way. One of his nieces said she loved my haircut. My hair was in one of Halle Berry's short haircut styles. His father and mother were very nice and asked me several questions. The father asked what I did for a living? I explained I had been a police sergeant with Dekalb County for ten years. He was very interested in my career and accomplishment within the police department. As I was talking, one of his sisters stopped me. She said, wait a minute, you have been a police officer for ten years; how old are you? I was thirty-eight years old. We realized that we were just a year apart, and her entire mood changed toward me. She was smiling and talking to me. She told me I did not look my age, and she thought I was close to her daughter's age of twenty-six. The dinner ended on a positive note. The relationship with his sisters was interesting. He was the youngest and only boy out of four children. He told me he was closest to his third sister Cathy because she was his favorite sister. A divorced mother with an adult son and daughter. We went out with her, laughed and had a great time. Then he suddenly started saying negative things about her. Some of his comments were very nasty and offensive. I was surprised at how he turned on her. They got in a bad argument and pulled out weapons on each other. He was the victim when he said his side of the story. He told me that she called me all kinds of names and didn't like me. I was hurt because I thought she was cool, and I did not say anything wrong about her. He changed to say that his oldest sister, Victoria, who is deceased, was his favorite sister, the one he loved the most. A mother of two adult sons and one juvenile-age son. They cracked jokes, and she kept it real. Victoria shared the same mother as William, Cathy, and Jessica. Victoria was a free spirit and loved all her sons dearly. I liked her energy and laugh. Then William would start saying negative and nasty things about her. His sister Jessica was the ace sister he loved the most in his words. Jessica was around him more than all the sisters. She was married with an adult daughter, Wanda, and an adopted son. I helped put together her graduation party for obtaining her nursing degree. We became very close, and I don't believe William liked that. We would tell her she said negative things about me, which I found false. I could not understand what was going on. He said he was the family's black sheep, and they didn't like him. I asked him why he did not date women in Macon. I never got an answer, just deflected from the question. A big red flag, but I continued the relationship. On another occasion, I met a baby girl. I learned she was born in October 2005, and it was his youngest daughter. I told myself this happened before I met him, and it was none of my business. He said he was not with the mother, and she was a one-night stand. After that situation, I asked him how many children he had, and he answered four. He had two boys and two girls from four different women. Although I would judge myself for having five baby fathers, I did not judge him. I did not inquire about the mothers of his children. During 2006, our relationship was off and on. He was very affectionate in public when the relationship was on, hugging and kissing me, holding my hand. He introduced me to friends or people he knew out in Macon as his girl. It didn't last long; if we had something negative going on between us, I would excuse it away. I didn't understand the nights I couldn't contact him. He revealed he was pledging to become an Omega Psi Phi fraternity member. I believe he crossed May 6, 2006, Spring chapter; he did not invite me. On May 5, the night before they crossed, he and his line brothers went to celebrate and asked me to come along. I met two of them as his friends, not knowing they were pledging with him. We met at the restaurant that hosted a Cinco De Mayo celebration. William disappeared once inside the restaurant, leaving me standing near the bar by myself. While I was standing there, one of the guys began holding a conversation with me. He asked me questions, thinking I was a single woman. I was confused because he was a friend of William's, and the other guys knew I was dating him. William must have seen what was happening and magically appeared behind me. He grabbed me on my waist, turned me around, and kissed my lips. The guy stepped back and said, oh, it's like that now. I could see the confusion on his face about who I was to William. I didn't read that deep into it. Did I want a long-distance relationship again? I decided to take a mental getaway trip to Bike Week in Myrtle Beach, South Carolina, with my friend Pat. I had never experienced anything like it. I was free to express myself with no judgment. On the five-hour road trip to Myrtle Beach, my friend Pat expressed that a particular gentleman wanted to make sure I came to bike week. She said his name was Toby. I assumed he was shy and didn't have the nerves to approach me. Traffic was at a standstill, and people were doing tricks on the motorcycles. We pulled into the parking lot, and I saw Toby standing there with a big smile. They said what happens in Myrtle Beach stays in Myrtle Beach. It was crazy fun. This situation in Myrtle has to be said. Ladies, you have to stay safe and watch your surroundings. I had fun until an unknown guy attempted to attack me in my hotel room. I shared a room with three other women. The only person I knew in the room was Pat. I didn't own a motorcycle and rode on the back of Toby or my friend Dean's motorcycle. Everyone was lining their motorcycles up to head out for dinner. I went to the room to get my purse. After I grabbed my purse and turned to leave my room, a guy walked through the door. I looked at him as if he didn't realize he had walked into the wrong room or maybe was looking for one of the other girls. I attempted to walk past him, and he grabbed me. I tried to snatch them away from him, and he tackled me to the bed. I started fighting him, but he was too strong. He grabbed my shorts, and I told him no as I pushed him. I said, what the fuck is wrong with you? I am a damn police officer. He immediately stopped, jumped up, and ran out of the room. I had to get myself together. I was so shaken and embarrassed that I had let this happen to me. Why did I leave the door partially open and get caught off guard? I ran outside to the group, who was ready to go. I was looking around to see if I could find the guy, but it was too many people. I jumped on the back of Toby's motorcycle and didn't tell anyone what had just happened to me. I thought the police officers would tease me for allowing it to happen. I am supposed to be aware of my surrounding. The situation bought back so many horrible memories that I decided to drink the pain away. I was so intoxicated that I could barely walk. I went to bed early that night in Toby's room because I was afraid to stay in my room. I told Pat what happened the next day, but I knew that guy had to be long gone from the area. Returned to Georgia, Toby and I began spending a lot of time together. I put William on the back burner because of the distance to his house. Toby and I realized the distance from our houses was about seven minutes. I was really into Toby mentally and physically. The chemistry was there, and he kept me smiling and laughing. After six months of me exclusively hanging out with him: he never referred to me as a girlfriend. I blamed myself because I should have expressed, I wanted a relationship. He was honest about not wanting a committed relationship; I knew I had to stop everything. I went on a cruise, and it was time to end it when I came back. It wasn't fair how I did it, but I must go cold turkey because I was addicted to him. I had planned a cruise on the Carnival Cruise line with the girls for Valentine's Day. I wanted to be in the middle of the ocean, away from any man I knew. I spent a lot of time sitting out on the deck just glazing into the ocean. It was so peaceful and serene. I noticed couples getting married or celebrating their anniversaries. In my heart, I wanted true love. I didn't know how to receive it. I was looking at my cellphone, which did not have a signal. Then suddenly it started ringing, and to my surprise, William called me. I hesitated at first, then answered. He said I wanted to wish you a Happy Valentine's Day and please call me when you get back to the United States. I want to talk and see you. I said to myself, this is a sign that he is the one I need to give him time. I was excited and ran to tell the girls about receiving a phone call in the middle of the ocean. No one's phone was working. When we returned to the United States, I contacted William while we drove back to Atlanta. He told me to stop in Macon, and he will bring me home the next day. My friends in the car kept saying; you never gave William a chance. He is good-looking, has a good job and seems very nice. I said, OKAY, ladies; I will give him a chance. We didn't reach Macon until 2:30 am, and he didn't answer the phone. Suppressing my feeling for Toby, who did not change his mind about committing to a relationship. We did not see each other regularly anymore. William called me the next day and asked to see me because he wanted to talk. I told him I would drive down to Macon, but I wasn't sure of a date. It was going on for four weeks, and I had not made the trip to Macon. William was not happy that I was putting him off. I knew Toby was not completely out of my system. In April, I met William at the Cracker Barrel in Macon, Georgia, to talk. He expressed that we never gave each other a fair chance to develop a relationship. He wanted to be exclusive with each other. I could not give him a yes right away. I told him I needed time to deal with my situation and let him know. Three weeks later, I called him and said, if you still want to try, I am ready to move forward with exploring a serious relationship. With that, I was 100 percent into making our relationship work. I called him the following day and got no answer. The next day no answer. He called me on the third day, and I explained that this was not how it would work. How do I get to know you if you go days without answering my calls? From that day on, we talked every day. Sometimes it was just a good morning or good night because work could be demanding. I spent the holidays with him and his family early in the relationship. We are having a conversation over the phone, and he reveals he is the pastor of a CME church. My heart stopped because I had sex with a pastor, and I was not his wife. I condemned myself right then and there. I asked him whether he preached on premarital sex. He was offended by the question. I didn't know how it works to date a pastor. I wish I had known from day one. I was like, at this point, what am I supposed to do but move forward. I asked whether there were any more surprises, and he responded no. Eventually, he introduced me to all of his children. He talked about and showed how much he loved his children. I accepted his children into my life. I saw their interaction with their dad and felt it was time to introduce my three youngest children to him. I knew he was a pastor, and I felt that I could trust him, be open, and not judge me. He had to travel a lot with the military and being a pastor. He asked me to accompany him on his business trips. I took off from work because I had unused vacation time and worked in an administrative position. I attended my first CME Convocation with him and attended at least two each year. Out of the ten years, I only missed one Convocation. He introduced me as his better half or lady to the church members. At his church, I was introduced as his friend initially, and then as time passed, I was assumed to be more than a friend. I attended his first church in Wadley, GA, Trinity CME church. The church members were very nice, and the choir was amazing. I was excited to learn about the CME church and its differences from the Baptist church. Each Sunday he preached, I would travel an hour to Macon, another hour and a half to his church, and then an hour back home. He would drive to and from church because I drove from Atlanta. As time progressed in the relationship, I began driving to and from church to allow him to prepare for his sermon, get into the mindset, and feel rested before the sermon. Listening to him preach began to draw me in more and more. We will discuss what he preached about then he will always ask, how did I do? What did you think? What was the message? I had to answer him, or he would respond with a sarcastic remark. His mother rode to church with us the majority of the time. I felt good energy from his family members, especially his mom and dad. I was impressed with the length of time (over 40 years) they had been married. I thought it reflected on the possibilities for William and me to have something long-term. The family fellowshipped together often with dinners, cookouts, movies, and more. They all had each other's back, churchgoers, very close. My children had attended my local church with no problems. They didn't like the long drive to his church, only meeting his children. I thought about moving to Macon to make things easier for him and me. First, I wanted to make sure I was vested at Dekalb County for twenty years before leaving. I was willing to give up my house and job. I would give up the rank of sergeant and become an officer inside the Bibb County Sheriff's Department. William contacted a friend who worked for the sheriff's department to guide me through hiring. I completed the physical agility test background package and scheduled my oral interview. He was encouraging me to move. I talked to my children, who expressed they did not want to move and graduate from their high school. I remember being in the military and my parents pulling me out of school and losing my friends. I couldn't do that to my children. I stopped everything with the hiring phrase. I submitted a letter to the hiring team withdrawing my application. He told me a friend and her girls were riding with us one Sunday. He said she was married but wanted to support him at his church. He introduced Kendra along with her two small daughters. One daughter's name stuck out, Cynthia, because it's close to my name, Cindy. Kendra and her daughters sat in the back seat, and I rode in the front with William. Kendra and I talked to each other as we drove to the church. She was charming, and her daughters were so sweet. We sat together at church on the second pew. After church Kendra and I were standing outside near William's vehicle when she said, I like you more than others. I never asked for clarification of her statement. However, I assumed she was happy with William choosing me. Different men and women rode to church with us, so I was not alarmed with Kendra riding to church with us. A few months later, I heard the congregation complain he had too many different women coming to the church. It did not look good. I believe that was why he wanted to move to another church. However, He wrote a letter requesting to move to a different church because the travel was too much. His request was honored. William was reassigned to a new church an hour away from his house. He did not preach every Sunday because the church members attended a different church every other Sunday. He said it was unfair to ask me to drive down every Sunday and insisted I come every other Sunday. I kept telling him I did not care. I felt like his lady. It was expected of me. I traveled with him on a Wednesday for bible study too. I shifted my life to make sure I was available for him. I didn't want the church members to think I wasn't supporting him. I did not ask for the title, first lady. However, the church members treated me as a first lady. When he finished preaching, I would gather his belongings such as his robe, bible, notepad, iPad, and water. I would turn on the air conditioner in the summer or the heat in the winter to make sure the car was ready for him. The ladies became very close to me and exchanged phone numbers. Several reached out to me about police-related situations or just talked about life. I did not speak about my relationship with William. I traveled with William and one of his coworkers, who he referred to as a true best friend, was Joseph. Joseph was a white male with who I had the best time hanging out. William was busy on his phone all of the time. Joseph and I had a thing for being on time, but William would show up at the last minute for our flights. He liked people to see him walking on the plane last. William was Joseph's boss per the rank structure in the Air Force. Joseph looked up to William because he knew how to speak to the ladies. On one training trip, we went to Reno, Nevada. Joseph did not come with us this time. William took me with him to the evening session of his training class on our first day there. After that day, I had the rental vehicle. I spent time exploring the city. I saw a tattoo business and wanted to know if they did temporary tattoos. I did not have any tattoos on my body but have thought about getting an ankle bracelet tattoo with my five children's names. While he was in training at the conference, I decided to surprise him with a tattoo of his name on my body. I told the lady I just wanted a temporary one to see how it looked instead of getting a permanent one. She stated she could only do a permanent tattoo. The other guys in the shop started asking me if he was the one but remember, it's permanent. I went back and forth in my head should I do it. I loved him and wanted to show him. I decided to get a tattoo of his name on my back. I told him I had a surprise for him, but he had to wait until after dinner. We found a place to eat in the casino at the hotel. I still had it covered, and he was like, okay, so what is my surprise? I turn away from him and lift my shirt back to show the bandage. He removed the bandage. I did not see his reaction, but I heard him say, wow. He hugged me and said, wow, that's deep. He said, you love me, and I was like, yeah. He pointed out this is permanent. He talked about he was going to get my name tattooed on him, which he never did. We were going back and forth about some time, and I turned to him and said, you don't own me, and his reply was, well, according to the name on your back, I do. I can't remember how long before my second tattoo of his Omega Psi Phi fraternity line name, PROMISE LAND. I tattooed them across my lower back. He would tell people about the tattoos and sometimes ask me to show them off. I thought I did a great thing honoring him and proving how much, I loved him. His niece, Brinna, said Cindy is the real one. She's the loyal one, Unc! I spent more time in Macon, Georgia, than in Atlanta. We were on good terms again.

I ignored a significant situation that happened early in the relationship. We had returned home from a trip. I was asleep for the night when my phone rang. I looked at the ID. It was William calling me. I kept saying hello, but he didn't answer me. Then I could hear the voice of a female fussing at him. I believe his phone was in one of the pockets of his jeans. He wore his jeans oversized. I sat up in my bed, and my heartbeat was so hard. I did not want to believe he was cheating on me, not a preacher. They were arguing about him not buying her anything from his trip. She was upset; he purchased a robe for himself. I called his house phone from my daughter Ashley's phone. I hear the female voice say, who is this bitch Ashley calling your fucking phone. He wasn't responding to her questions and picked up the house phone and asked who she was? He told me nobody was at his house. I screamed you are a liar. You accidentally called me on your phone. I could hear your conversation and her asking you questions. I kept calling your name, so I called your house phone from Ashley's phone. He ignores me and goes into a panic, searching for his cellphone. She was screaming, who was Ashley. I could tell when he located his cellphone because he hung it up. I called his sister Jessica, crying, telling her what had happened. She kept saying I am so sorry, Cindy. I will call him and talk to him. I told her it was over between us. I cried myself to sleep from another heartbreak. The following day William called my phone, and I didn't answer. He kept sending text messages which I ignored. He texted it was his sister Cathy at his house. According to William, Cathy did not like me, so I could not verify whether she was at his home. He kept apologizing and telling saying I love you. Please talk to him. He sent an email to my job saying all the right things to get me back. As of today, I am sure it was Kendra at his house. I have called his home on occasions, and Kendra has answered the phone. He always returned my phone calls. I wasn't alarmed because she liked me better than the other ones, a family friend and she was married with two children. We had ridden in his car twice to support William's preaching at his church. He told me he needed to speak to me about a problem on one occasion. A church member's husband accused him of having an affair. It was ironic; I remember her singing a solo and his reaction when she sang. He sat in the pulpit with his eyes closed and waved his hands. He didn't have the same response to the other women singing. Was I being paranoid? I was confused. I told William I had no problem speaking with him. That meeting never happened, and William made sure of that. I believe he was testing my reaction. Things were getting out of hand at the second church, and he wanted a new church. It was time for him to grow to a larger congregation. He moved to his second church in Hawkinsville, Georgia. We attended his home church on holidays or when he didn't preach. Later in the relationship, I visited William's home church, but I had never been downstairs in the fellowship hall. The church members were hosting a dinner. I noticed a wall filled with old pictures of William and his children; I looked closer and saw Kendra. He said she had been a family friend for years. I didn't think anything of it because I have innocent photos of my male friends. I had a habit of discounting my feeling away. We spent time outside of the church at family and friend functions. Jessica asked me to coordinate her wedding vow renewal on September 6; putting my birthday aside, I agreed. Winona was the event planner and decided to help me. As all wedding have their stressors, this wedding had its incidents. On September 5, we set up the venue then Jessica, Wanda, Winona, and I went out to eat dinner. Jessica stated she had something to share with me about William during the dinner but only after the wedding. Winona responded you know I will fight your brother about her. Jessica responded I would fight you about my brother. Winona asked even if he was wrong. She replied, yes, I have done it before. William distanced himself from me during and after the ceremony. Winona and I were sitting in the car about to head back to Atlanta when Jessica approached us. She looked at me and only said thank you for everything. Several years later, I discovered William gave his furniture to Kendra instead of Wanda. I believe Jessica intended to expose William cheating with Kendra. I remember she said no matter if he was wrong, she would fight for him. I continued to support William and stayed away from their sibling rivalry. A family function for Memorial day turned into a family brawl. I volunteered to work my off day as a shift supervisor with the Dekalb County police department when we received a disturbing 911 call. A young child stuck on a grill. My thought processed a child hit by a vehicle stuck in the car grill. Upon arrival, I observed a white SUV near the townhouse outside stairs, an egg-shaped cooking grill with a small child lying across it. The child was non-responsive and smoking. The hot grill wedged between the SUV and townhouse. We could not reach the child and needed to push the vehicle off the grill. Two additional police officers arrived on the scene, and with strength, we moved the car. Then it started rolling back down the driveway when I noticed it was in neutral gear. I leaped across the front passenger seat, pressed the breaks with one hand, and put it in the park position. Another police officer and I removed him. His body was smoking, and I observed ribs fully cooked. The fireman arrived on the scene and took over attending to him. I knew he was deceased. After everything was under control, I noticed the officers had difficulty processing the loss. We went back to the precinct and shredded many tears. I called William to express the pain and sorrow I felt. He prayed with me and said he would see me later and at my aunt's cookout. I arrived at my aunt's house early to decompress from the trauma at work. My aunt and I sat outside in the backyard sipping wine, and I cried again. William, Cathy, his nephew, and Wanda arrived at the house. Later that evening, my aunt informed me that her friend complained about William touching her breast and left the cookout. I did not need more trauma or drama and did not want to believe the woman. I got up the nerve to confront him, and he denied everything. He became upset with me for accusing him and walked away. I explained to my aunt that he denied everything calling the woman a liar. I stayed away from William until the fight broke out. I assumed my aunt told my uncle about the incident involving William and the woman. My uncle confronted William in the front yard then I heard my aunt screaming, STOP fighting. I ran out of the house and observed them on the ground fighting. Everyone came outside, attempting to break the fight up. They both stood up, and my uncle headed toward his vehicle parked down the street. William kept saying he had no right to touch you as a little girl and needed to be taught a lesson and honor me. Someone screamed my uncle was going to get his gun. William's gun was inside my car. I quickly ran to my car to hide his weapon while William, his nephew, and Wanda jumped in the car. I wanted to leave as soon as possible before anything else happened. Cathy was following my uncle, trying to catch up to my car. My uncle did not know my address, and it was dark outside. Cathy informed us he turned around. I had a flashback when I was sixteen years old, and my uncle was involved in an incident with one of our cousins. The incident resulted in a fistfight, gunfight, and my cousin dying. My uncle received ten years in jail for involuntary manslaughter. The day was an emotional roller coaster. Was

William manipulating the situation to cover up for touching the woman? I wanted to believe him because this was a delicate subject for me. However, his family said the woman had to be lying because they were together on deck with him. My aunt called the next day to inform me of the words exchanged between William and my uncle. He was not welcome back to her home because it traumatized her family, and his actions were not becoming a pastor. I chose not to explain William's side of the story because my aunt did not know what had happened to me. His military coworkers knew me, and I went on an impromptu mini vacation with eight of them to Florida. I realized that my cell phone did not work at the beach house. William had my complete attention hanging out inside the pool for hours. Afterward, William and I grilled the food for everyone while the other ladies kept our cups full of alcohol. However, one female and one male coworker came solo and did not hook up. I did notice William was a little friendly with females who came solo. She was married with two children. I thought to myself, why invite me if she came solo based on how he acted towards her after having several drinks. I acted like it didn't bother me, but I was pissed. I worked on hiding my emotions. I am sure he knew in my body language that I was not happy. I should have paid attention to his reactions of not caring about it. Other people noticed it and looked over at me for my response, the beginning of me suppressing my hurt when it came to him. I went upstairs to our room to get myself together. About fifteen to twenty minutes later, William came to our room, hugging and kissing me, apologizing if he offended me. Someone said something about his disrespectful actions and corrected him. I told him that was not cool. I went back downstairs with him, but I noticed he stayed far away from her for the rest of the trip. Later that year, I went to a company picnic with William, and he was talking to some guys from his unit I had never met. I was over talking to Joseph and his son. I noticed the female from the mini vacation was there with her husband, and she was extremely friendly to me. I kept my eye on her, or maybe I should have been keeping my eye on William. We went on two cruises to Cancun and Nassau, taking personal and professional photos. Still, he never posted them on social media. When he felt me pulling away, he would discuss marriage and what ring I wanted. I felt alive and excited about getting married. After two failed marriages and over forty years old, I wanted things to work between us and needed to forgive him. I initially went to the ring store to get an idea of what I wanted and decided on a princess-style cut ring. He suggested my girlfriends and I attend the wedding expo in Atlanta. William and I agreed to meet with Shelly, our wedding coordinator off Buford highway, to look at the first venue and pick out wedding colors. He was traveling from Macon, which was a two-hour drive. He called to say he was on his way. Winona, Shelly, and I headed to the venue. He called several times as he was traveling to update his time. After thirty minutes from when he was supposed to arrive, I called to ensure he was okay. No answer. Once we finished the venue tour and picked out the colors, I called him again. He answered the phone saying something had happened at work, and he could not come. Things did add up, but I didn't make a fuss because I wouldn't choose the venue. He kept apologizing for disappointing me. He promised not to miss any more dates. We discuss finding a venue between Atlanta and Macon for our families. He gave me the list of guys he wanted as his groomsmen and best man. His sister Jessica was one of the bridesmaids and my best friends, daughters, and other friends. All the ladies went to David's Bridal and tried on the dresses I picked out. The dresses looked beautiful on all the ladies' body types. His sister told me about an art gallery in Forsyth, GA, for our reception. I met with the owner of the art gallery twice about my vision. This location could only hold the reception, and I needed to find a wedding venue. I wanted to do my wedding and reception in the same place, and this place was big enough. The owner said that's ironic because I'm looking at converting the other portion of the building into a wedding venue. Our vision of how the bride would walk down the aisle lined up. I never walked down the aisle and was excited about the completion date. Our wedding would be the first or second in the new wedding venue. The location was perfect since it was thirty-five minutes from Atlanta and thirty minutes from Macon. William said he would give me the money to secure our date. Everything was moving along great. No ring yet. William and I visited my dad and momma two at their house. My dad told me William asked for a hand in marriage, and he gave him the okay. I didn't know that was why he wanted to go over there. His niece called me and said, hey, I know what you're getting for Christmas, she was very excited, and I was like, oh Lord, no, please let it be a surprise. Not sure what my surprise was because I never received it. Did I think it was an engagement ring? Yes, I did, and no, I did not receive one yet. We were making a lot of planning for a wedding but no official proposal. William told everyone we were getting married in September and wanted them to attend. The relationship takes a nosedive when William and Jessica have an explosive argument on Thanksgiving Day, 2014. I spent the day with my family and went down later that evening to Macon. We were at his parent's house visiting with the family. The family members at the house were his mom and dad, sister Jessica, her husband, sister Victoria, niece Wanda, his oldest son, and two small children. William had a few drinks before I arrived. I could see he was feeling relaxed. A discussion was between William, Victoria, and Jessica about Wanda returning his vehicle with a full gas tank. Not sure when it shifted to relationships and hints of his infidelity. He became agitated, cursing and fussing with Jessica because she defended her daughter. Jessica was so upset that she had a panic attack. William's father ordered everyone to the front room while having a private conversation with William behind closed doors. I was in the front with the family, trying to calm Jessica down. William entered the room, saying some very hurtful things to Jessica again. Jessica's husband jumped in, giving a few choice words to William, defending Jessica. I escorted William outside to calm him down because I knew the alcohol was talking. He wanted his second car home and told me to drive it. I told his son to ride with me because William was drinking. William jumped in his vehicle and sped off from the house. Wanda stopped me by grabbing my hand and looking me in the eyes. Auntie, you deserve better than him. He is no good, and there is another woman whose name starts with a K. I did not want to believe her. Still, I remember locating a Father's Day card in his drawer a few days before, Kendra. The card was the same Father's Day card I gave him. He said it was a mistake and it belonged to his neighbor. I didn't believe him, but I had excused things away so much that I was numb. I asked her name Kendra, and she replied yes. I walked away, got in the car, and drove to his house with his son. I tried to smile and have a conversation with his son because he witnessed everything.

I wanted to cry so bad, but why. I did not want to accept it. I have been with him for almost ten years, off and on. People knew we were getting married. I was too embarrassed to walk away. I did want to go back to Atlanta that night. His niece called me as I drove back to his house to ensure I was okay. She told me other things he did and that I should leave him. The lady Kendra lived about five minutes away from him. I arrived at the house and told William I was driving back home. He started screaming and crying. I was leaving him. How could I believe them over him? I am his woman and should have his back. Cindy, you have hurt me to the core. I thought you loved me, Cindy. I thought about what he had told me. His family tells lies about him because he does not help them. I knew Wanda could not make up the name Kendra, but I stayed there anyway. I didn't want another failed relationship. I fell asleep and woke up the next morning to leave. He was sober and in a better mood. I kissed him goodbye and headed back home. I was in my head making everything make sense. I can fix this because I would not bring drama into our relationship. My friends and family kept asking about the wedding. I am a single mother of five children. I just had to make it work. I decided not to return to Macon for a while. I made excuses because I could not come down and only speak with him over the phone. His niece confirmed the information because she felt comfortable talking about everything. She was distraught with how William talked about her and her mom. She told me that Kendra had been over to his house if I ever saw macaroni and cheese in his refrigerator. We were approaching Christmas 2014, and things were better between William and me; however, I was skeptical of anything he told me. I told him I had to work on Christmas day. He said it was okay and we could get together on another day to exchange gifts. He was not acting himself, and I knew something was going on. I believe it was December 27, 2014; I did something I had never done. I popped up at my man's house unannounced. I called my best friend and asked if she wanted to ride down to Macon with me because I believe William has a woman at his house. I told her I had on sweatpants and my hair was in a ponytail. That was code we might have to fight him. I picked her up, dressed in sweatpants with her hair in a ponytail. I called his niece to let her know I was driving down and could you go by the house. She confirmed as we were pulling on his street. I gave her time to leave the area before I pulled up. I didn't know if he would fight me, but I didn't care. I thought about him being a black belt and decided to respond calmly. I knocked on the door but was not expecting his son to be at the house. My game plan changed quickly. I will not harm his child mentally or anyone in the house. I heard his son say, oh no, under his breath. I saw a nice Sunday dinner on the table and a macaroni and cheese dish. Yes, Kendra was there. She walked out of the kitchen and was surprised to see me. I said Hey Kendra, how are you. She replied, "Hey Cindy, how are you? "She walked over to the sink and continued to wash the dishes. I walk into the kitchen with her. I asked Kendra what her relationship with William was? She raised her hand and stated, we are engaged and getting married. I replied, wow, we are engaged to be married too. When is your wedding date? She said it was supposed to have been this past October, but we didn't get married. I said we are getting married next year on September 12. I have his name tattooed on my back. When I showed her the tattoo, she started screaming Bill wake up. She looked at me and said I had a feeling he was cheating again. My best friend posted between the front door and kitchen, making sure nothing happened. William started walking into the kitchen with his chest poked out to scare me. I turned to him with his house key in my hand. I said I hope she is worth losing me and handed him his key. I walked past him and walked over to his son, leaving him and Kendra in the kitchen. I told his son I loved him, apologized to him for witnessing this, and wished him the best. He thanked me, and I started walking toward the front door. Kendra came out of the kitchen and grabbed my hand. She looked at me and asked if we could talk outside. I said yes, very calming. William started walking behind us, and she decided not to talk to me. I had her phone number. I texted her later that she could talk to me anytime; I would tell her everything. William screamed at me to get out of his house. My best friend and I left his house. As I began to think about what I had just experienced, I cried. I didn't comprehend what I had just experienced. William was my fiancé; I was in love with him. Why is he at his house with her? He calls me and says, why did you do that? Why did you come to my house? You are wrong about that. I said I hope it was worth it because you hurt me to the core. I have been faithful to you and would never hurt you like this. I hung the phone in his face. Fifteen minutes later, he calls me again, apologizing and asking me to forgive him. I hung up the phone again. I ignored the calls the rest of the night. He started texting me. No response from me. I believe his niece told the family what happened that night. I do not remember if I called his father or if his father called me the next day. He tells me he and his wife appreciate me, I know you are hurting, but you are a very good woman. I hate that my son did this to you, and you deserve better. I have told my son to stop playing games with women. I wish you the best. We hung up. His father was always nice and would have life talks with me. I reached out to Kendra to see if she was ready to talk. She assured me she would return my call, but she never did. I was attempting to process the last nine-plus years of my life. His niece kept giving me updates about William and was remorseful of his actions. She told me she had not seen or heard from Kendra.

I celebrated New Year with some friends trying to forget about William. Instead, he called me to say he would spend New Year's Eve with his children at church. He wanted to wish me Happy New Year and be willing to talk to him again one day. I told his niece I would talk to him if he agreed to counsel. Another week went by before I was willing to meet with him in a public place. He agreed to enter counseling and do right by me. I wanted to throw my hands up and just walk away from everything. Thinking about how many years I invested and how embarrassing to walk away now. I am almost fifty years old and trying to start something new was not in the cards. I've been with this man. Okay, he had an affair or cheated on me. I know people have worked through situations like this, and so can I. He was willing to go to counseling and work things out. I am going to push forward in our relationship. We started counseling in February 2015; he admitted cheating on me with our counselor Dr. Mitchell. We had to write a letter to each other. He wrote me a letter about how things happened between Kendra and him. The letter talked about their friendship. That one thing led to another, and that it only happened twice two years ago. I was open and honest about how I felt. He gave us assignments, and one was to purchase and read the book the Five Love Languages. We needed to start there as we worked through his infidelity. He started the marriage counseling sessions because we were willing to move forward with the relationship. His niece said, well, whatever happened, he must have decided because I have not seen Kendra. We would eat after leaving the church, but he changed our plans this Sunday. He said he had something to do at work. I headed back to Atlanta but decided to ride by his house and saw her vehicle parked in the driveway. I didn't say anything to him until we were in front of our marriage counselor. He said Kendra stopped by to pick up her property, and the other vehicle was the mother of his youngest child. He mentioned that he had a two-week drill in the field. I said, during this time, we needed to do some soul searching about our relationship because his niece told me she saw him with Kendra and her daughter at his parent's house. He agreed. The family experienced a horrific event, a death. On March 8, I went to church in Perry, GA, but I didn't ride with William because he had an event at his job. However, his mom rode with me to church and hosted this year's annual choir revival. I could not attend the revival after church because I committed to attending a baby shower in Atlanta. His mother was staying at the church and was riding back home with her husband. Before I left, she asked to call her husband from my phone to see how far he was from the church before I headed back. After a brief conversation, I hugged his mom and headed to the baby shower. I didn't stay long at the baby shower because I felt overwhelmed and wanted to go home. Thinking about my relationship with William, who I no longer trusted, seeing those vehicles at his house. Wondered if he had convinced Kendra to take him back, going to counseling, and being willing to marry him. I would seriously do some soul searching while he was gone for two weeks. The phone ringing broke my thoughts. It was his sister Jessica who was screaming and crying. Daddy is gone; he is gone, then hung up. I attempted to call William to find out what was going on, but he did not answer. I called his niece, and she said her granddaddy died after he completed the solo of his favorite song. She said the choir returned to their seat in the congregation for the next choir to sing. He sat down and then slumped over in the pew. They started calling his name; Jessica tried to help her dad and called 911. The ambulance rushed him to the hospital, where he was pronounced dead. I was devasted and started crying. He died in front of his wife and oldest daughter. Their father was an amazing man. I called William, who was crying uncontrollably. I told him I loved him, and he called me back after the hospital. The hospital was about an hour and forty-five minutes away from me. I asked his sister if she needed me to drive back down. She replied a lot is going on; just give him time, which was understandable. Well, I found out Kendra was with him at the hospital. I convinced myself it wasn't a big deal that she was there because I knew about her; she's still a family friend. She's there to be supportive. It was devastating because I was building the courage to walk away from our situation. I can't leave him now. That would be selfish after losing his dad suddenly and at his church. When I heard my phone ringing, I snapped out of my thoughts and looked at the caller ID to show William. He cried and repeatedly said, I am in my daddy's car. He sounds like he is five years old. He was crying so hard. My daddy is gone. I asked what you needed me to do? He wanted me to come to Macon. I need you, Cindy. Please come down, and I said OKAY. I picked up a few things if I decided to stay overnight and headed to his parent's house. Well known in Macon, and the number of people at the house proved it. I immediately located William with several frat brothers; he reached out to me and started hugging me. He kept saying thank you for coming down. I love you so much; he wouldn't let me go as he continued to cry. We went inside the house so I could see his mom. I hugged and cried with her. He asked me to stay because he did want to be alone. I had enough time to take off at my job. I stayed for two weeks, commuting to Atlanta. I was helping with the funeral arrangements for his father. I discovered he had six children with six different mothers during the funeral planning. He also had three mothers pregnant at the same time while being married to one of them. I was there with him and the family to select the casket and the clothing. The grandchildren Wanda and Dexter oversaw the writing of the eulogy. Everybody wanted it to say this or say that. They wanted all their photos in the program. It was becoming overwhelming for them. I stepped in and asked to take over the program. I contacted my friend Shelly who agreed to do the program for me. I took care of William, drove back home to check on my children, and met with Shelly twice to complete the programs. Once the family approved the programs, I drove back down to Macon because William did not want to be alone. The next day drove back to Atlanta to pick up the programs. I stayed busy at his mom's house, ensuring everyone was fed and okay. Finally, people started telling me to sit down and rest because I looked exhausted. The mother of William's youngest son approached me to ask if we were still together. I told her yes, and she said, great, because I did not care for Kendra. I was confused by the question and thought about her son's age. William and Kendra were together when she got pregnant with his son. I am sure Kendra did not care for her. William saw us talking and sent a text message not to talk to her because she was messy. I didn't want to disrespect him and politely excused myself from the conversation. It was an honor for Bishop Johnson to fly in from Texas, meet with his mom, and agree to preach at his father's funeral. William introduced me to the bishop as his better half. Later, one of his church members told me that after William introduced me to the bishop and walked away, he mumbled she is for now. The statement was hurtful, and I wanted to say the hell with all of this. I had to take my feelings out of this. The night before the funeral, I talked with William about Kendra attending the funeral. I told him that I was okay with her and understood she had been a family friend for years. I wanted to make sure he was okay. The children spent the night at his house. On the morning of the funeral, I woke up his children to get dressed then I attended to William. I picked out everything he wanted to wear when he honored his father. I had to dress him because he was in disbelief and physically struggled. He had cried most of the night, but he pulled himself together in front of his children. We arrived at his mom's house. I told William I knew we were not married yet and would not ride in a limo. When she arrived, the family was not very welcoming to Kendra and didn't want her bothering William. His children blocked the door to William's room while he prayed and reflected on his father's life. Kendra and I spoke to each other. The limos arrived, and the family lined up next to the vehicles. I jumped in the vehicle with Jessica's best friend and lined up as the fourth vehicle behind the limos. I could see Kendra standing near the limo that William was sitting inside. Still, I overheard the family members telling her to move away from the vehicle. She was visibly upset because someone overheard her fussing about riding in the family limo with William. The limos began to pull off, and Kendra stood on the sidewalk. I couldn't understand why she was upset. Things are over between you and William. If I am not in the limo, why are you upset. I believe she jumped into the van carrying the pallbearer. Once at the church, I located William's children and made sure they stayed together. Drake's mother personally walked over to me. She asked that I take care of her baby because he was upset about losing his grandfather. The children walked in with me, and we sat directly behind William and his mom. William mainly attended to his mother while I took care of his children. I could feel the tension of his family towards Kendra. I did not live in Macon and did not know why. I overheard someone say why she tried so hard to be in his face. Kendra attempted to sit next to William at the repast. I did not care because I was helping his mother. I sat down with William's ex-wife, her sister, and William's daughter to eat and conversate with them. The repast was not the time or place for drama. I headed back home the next day. His sister or niece told me people wanted to see how Kendra and I would act towards each other. I am happy to say we did not give them a show. I had nothing against Kendra. We fell in love with the same guy. William and I are working through his infidelity. In April, The bishop chose William as the guest speaker at the next Annual Convocation Conference. Honored by request, William asked me to join him at the conference. Bishops and Pastors were flying across the world to attend the conference.

William's mom and I sat on the front row with the bishops' wives. After the conference, we had to leave back out of town to North Carolina for a training class with his job. Since I did not have time to drive back home, I packed enough clothes for two weeks. I left some of my clothing items in my pink bag at William's house to repack my suitcase to head to North Carolina. After a successful trip to the conference, we return home to his mother's house. I received a phone call from Wanda asking why Kendra called me about a pink Victoria bag? I was like, huh? She's like, yes, Kendra says she's going to burn this house down or what not? I was like, what? She went to William's house to pick up my bag, and she will bring it to me. I look for William in the front room on the phone, fussing with someone. He is upset and making statements. I will call the police if you don't leave my house now. What are you doing at my house? I'm going to call the police; you need to get out of my house. I need my key back. Why are you there? Why are you touching Cindy's stuff or whatnot? I ask, what is going on? He says she still had a key. She shouldn't have been in my house. I told her it was over, and she was at my house, and there was some craziness. William jumps in his dad's pick-up truck and leaves for about ten minutes. He returned, acting as if nothing had happened. He said I just couldn't believe she did that. I think Kendra is obsessed with William, or he is still lying to us. I ask myself, why am I here? I could not answer myself. We go to Charlotte, North Carolina, and things are better on the way up there. William and I had looked at some houses and land to build a house. We drove to this training in a military van. Joseph and one other coworker drove up with us. I stayed at the hotel until they came back to pick me up for lunch. I received a phone call from Jessica checking on me from the latest incident with Kendra and my pink bag. I say things were good and we looked at some other houses. She said she didn't understand because "Ken" made it like they were still together. I decided to apologize to Kendra for bringing her into William and I relationship. She responded I was not in a relationship with William. She told me she was marrying William; they have a bank account and a key to his house. I was about to tell her. Well, that's ironic because I'm here in North Carolina with him now. We looked at houses together, and I have a key to his house, but that's messy. I just said, okay, she's got some serious issues. Not knowing William was lying to both of us. I was about to send William a text message when I received one from him. He asked if I had sent something to Kendra. I responded, yes. I did the woman thing, and I apologize to Kendra for bringing her into our relationship. He says, what did you do that? Why did you stir stuff up again? It's nothing between us. You should just leave that alone. I said, well, I'm just being open with you. I reached out to her. I didn't feel right about how he reacted, and Kendra was texting like they were still together. He returned to the room, and I acted like everything was good. He said we were going out to eat with the guys tonight. While we were eating, I received a phone call from Jessica saying Kendra was talking and showing pamphlets of the same house. She told her they were purchasing a house together. I wanted to cry because I felt so stupid. I was holding it together, but I had to leave the table. I went to the restroom to let it out and pretended I was not feeling well. Joseph could see in my face I was crying because he kept looking at me and asking if I was okay. We were heading back to the hotel, and William needed another toothbrush. We stopped at a drug store, and I jumped out to go into the store because I did not want to be in the car with him. While I was looking for the toothbrush, Joseph came around the aisle and asked, was I okay? He said, Cindy, don't say anything, but I think you should leave William alone because he does not appreciate you. I was shocked because Joseph always agreed with anything William said, but maybe he had enough. I knew something was not right. On the drive back to Georgia, William sat in the last row of the van on his phone and ignored me most of the time. He had a nasty attitude towards me. I could not wait to get out of that van. I needed to be far away from him. From the trip in April, things were touch and go between us. I expressed how I felt about the North Carolina trip back in the van and the text message with Kendra. Still, I never told him about the house situation. Jessica and Wanda were communicating more with me about conversations with William. He expressed he wanted to marry me. I let my guard back down and went house hunting with him again. We decided to build and move forward with a down payment on the lot in a gated community. We were still going to marriage counseling, and I was ready to discuss the current situation. William was still all over the place about losing his father, and I excused his actions away. I was listening to his niece and sister about his love for me. I thought maybe I was tripping. I went to church every other Sunday. The lady read the church announcements that the pastor's appreciation day was May 31, which fell on Sunday; I attended church. I will not miss his pastor's appreciation day; he started acting stand-offish and didn't spend Memorial Day with me. I was thinking about not going to his appreciation because of his actions. We did not speak all day on Saturday, which confirmed I was not going. Then on Sunday, he called saying he had a hard day yesterday, missing his dad. He apologized for not calling me. I told him I loved him and wished him a better day. Then Jessica reached out to me and asked if I would be at his appreciation day today. I told her I wasn't, but I would look crazy to the congregation not coming to my man celebration. My thoughts were all over the place. We were in marriage counseling, and I never cheated on him. I didn't tell my dad that I caught him cheating and how the whirlwind happened. I gave him ten years, well, a true eight years, because of the back and forth of the first two years. I gave you time and time again, which I hadn't in the past relationships other than my high school sweetheart. I asked myself the following questions. How did he hold this charade up for this length of time? How did I not, or why didn't I see that things weren't adding up? I asked specifically when we first met. Why didn't he date anyone in Macon? His response now, it's too much drama here with these women. He manipulated Kendra, his siblings, his nieces, and me. Family members finally told me to leave him alone, but I was so deep in love at that point. It will be okay if I do right and don't bring drama. If I were getting close to one of my female relatives, he would tell me they do not like me and make up a story about why. Memories of William in the hospital because of his medical conditions. The incident happened a year or two into the relationship, and I should have been at the hospital. Jessica said you don't need to come. I just wanted to let you know if he didn't answer the phone. I could hear many people in the background, including his children. Years later, I found out why he did not want me to come down. It was a hospital discharge paper signed by Kendra Pounds at his house. Things started to add up backward for me. I asked myself, why did he bring me into his mess. Why did those females in his family cover for him that long? Kendra and I were both in his life.

Chapter 7

On May 31, I showed up at the church to surprise him with his pastor's appreciation day celebration. It was a surprise for all, including Kendra. What happened that day started a downward spiral. After talking to William about how much he missed his father, his sister encouraged me to be there. I drove an hour and forty-five minutes to church, arriving simultaneously with a church member. She said it was good to see you. I came to support Pastor Pounds and surprise him. She thought that was a wonderful thing to do. I greeted the church members as I made my way to the second pew. I also noticed several church members from his home church located in Macon. I picked up the program and saw a photo of him. I sent a text message to William saying I am here to support you, baby. I believe he was in the parking lot when he texted me; the church members complained about not having the money and canceled the appreciation day. I replied I had the program in my hand. I saw Kendra walk through the door along with his youngest daughter. We made eye contact and then looked away. His daughter gave me a big hug and then sat next to me. Kendra was holding it together. Kendra sat down on the same pew as I, with his daughter separating us. William was exchanging text messages with Kendra because she had her phone in her hand. I could feel the anxiety and hurt in my body, but I had to stay calm. Kendra's leg was moving so fast that I knew she was giving William a piece of her mind. I received a text message from William; his mom slipped and fell. He wanted me to help her. His mother was home in Macon, an hour away. I texted Jessica, sitting next to the pastor, and inquired about their mom. I asked if her mother needed me? She responded no because Wanda was there with her, and she was okay. I responded to William that Wanda was there. His attempt to make me leave did not work. Kendra walked out of the sanctuary towards the restroom when the guest preacher spoke about William. I know she was trying to deal with the situation as I. He has shamed us in front of these church members. Now he was in the hot box. I could only imagine what was going through everyone's minds. The program was over, and we headed to the kitchen to eat and fellowship. I attended to William's daughter as she helped herself with the food. We sat down to eat across from Jessica, her husband, and their son. Kendra sat down with one chair, separating us. Jessica looked at her then me and stated, you two need to talk. While looking at Jessica stating I reached out to Kendra and then turned towards her, but she never returned my call. Kendra said we could talk now. I stood up to walk outside to the parking lot. Kendra stood up and walked towards William. She returns, stating he won't come with us. Jessica said, no, Kendra, just you and Cindy. Kendra replied He needs to be there because he is the reason for all of this. I had all I could take with the situation. I walked over to William, handed him his gift, gave him a church hug, and headed home. I sat in my vehicle for a minute before letting the tears flow. My body was shaking and releasing the hurt. I felt like I was in a twilight zone. Why I could not accept the fact that he is a liar. While driving home, I received a text message from Kendra, and she added William to the text message thread. I can't remember the exact words, but it was something about him not being truthful. Kendra mentioned meeting at William's house, and we all discussed what was going on. I declined and text I was going home. Wanda and I texted briefly, but she informed me they were at his mom's house. I made it home. I just wanted this all to be a bad dream. Eventually, Kendra and I exchanged informational text messages throughout the evening and night. Kendra texted that what he did in the dark would come to light, and he waited until she was gone to make her seem crazy. We both were in love with him. When I received information my aunt Tan had passed away. Kendra sent her condolences and blessings. I sent her blessings in return. The text messages ended. William and I had a counseling and a tattoo session in Atlanta. I went to the counseling session by myself and explained everything that had occurred the day prior. During the session, Dr. Mitchell wanted me to focus on healing myself. After his tattoo session, William called, begging me to meet him in the parking lot of Tanger Mall off highway I-75; he was on his way back to Macon. Please allow him to explain himself; I agreed to meet him there, only to listen. I told Winona that I would go ahead and meet with him. It might have been about two o'clock in the afternoon. He kept apologizing, telling me I had been good to him. I deserve better from him. He said I could not turn off his love for Kendra like that, but he was in love with me. I asked for honesty, that's all. You are finally telling me the truth. He states I want to marry you badly. I want to give you two weeks of separation, and he would not contact me while I thought about our relationship. He apologized for all the stuff that had happened and wanted to move forward. He wanted to continue premarital counseling. He tells me I was always a good person and the best thing ever happened to him. He did bad things; I didn't clarify the bad things; I just assumed his cheating ways. He has hurt Kendra and me. He goes on to say; you are still here for him. I've always treated him like a king, and he wanted the opportunity to love me. He repeats he did love me. Then he started crying and getting very emotional to the point he struggled to talk. He asked me to think about us getting married in September. He said to think about it while he's out of town. He returns on June 5; then, he had to turn back around and fly to Dallas for a church conference. He asked if I could pick him up from the airport on June 5 and the following Friday from his Dallas trip. He hugged me, and we left the parking lot. I called Winona to tell her I was okay. He wanted to continue counseling and get married in September. It was up to me to make the decision. I thought he showed his feelings; he was sincere and wanted to continue premarital counseling. I believe we can make this work; he broke down. He was very emotional; he took responsibility for cheating and hurting me. He took the Groom airport shuttle from Macon to Hartfield-Jackson airport. On June 5, I picked him up from the airport and drove him back home. I said, let's do 6/12 instead of 9/12. Just flip the numbers. We can do the big wedding on September 12. We must be open and honest during our counseling sessions. That was the last time I saw William. I thought that maybe Kendra had left him. That's why he wants to be with me now. During this decision, I received a lot of inside feedback from Jessica and Wanda about conversations with William. They told me he wanted to be with me, and he broke things off with Kendra. It has been ten years. I am beating myself up about going through with getting married at the courthouse. I had to go to New Jersey for my aunt Fan's funeral when William was in Dallas. I rented a car to drive to New Jersey with Cortney, Gia, and my cousin. While I was in New Jersey, William called to tell me he was boarding the plane and would call before they took off. He said it was raining bad, and I'll call you when I get to Dallas. We exchanged I love you and hung up. He would check on me before he delivered his sermon. He called to let me know he was out to dinner with Bishop Johnson and other preachers. I told him we were driving back to Georgia on the 9th because I had my annual police in-service training on June 10 and June 11. We texted instead of talking to each other on my drive back to Georgia because of the phone reception. We talked about still getting married at the courthouse on June 12. I called Bibb County to check the hours of operations at the courthouse. What was the cut-off time for marriages on Friday? On June 10, I was at training and received text messages about picking him up from the airport on the 12th. I couldn't understand why he kept making sure I did not forget to pick him up from the airport. I was thinking about the time it takes to get on the road from the airport and make it back to Macon before the courthouse closes. Do you honestly think we will make it to the courthouse in time? He agreed it's close if we get stuck in traffic. I asked whether we needed to revisit another day. His response was we would discuss it. I was in limbo, but it was my thought process. He rushed me off the phone because he had to go to preach. He said everything went well in Dallas. The conference was great, and he did a good job. He said he was packing, and I will see you tomorrow. I was on the phone with a close friend who likes a brother around 10 pm. I was half asleep, sounding crazy on the phone. You must've been asleep. I replied, yes, call you tomorrow. I remember hanging up the phone and falling back to sleep. That was the last conversation before my phone rang at 1:06 am. It was a 478 number in the Macon area, but I didn't recognize it. I answered the phone, It was William, and he sounded like he was in a panic. I was half asleep, and I can't remember the exact words he said but what woke me up was him saying Kendra shot herself. I asked, "What are you talking about?" I looked at the phone again, looking at the unknown phone number; I asked again, what are you talking about? Repeating his words, "She shot herself?" I sat up in my bed, trying to get my barons. I asked whether the police were there; yes, they were here. I'm on my way; he says, please hurry, please hurry. I go into my third daughter's room; she doesn't sleep at night. She was awake; I said, Hey, something happened at William's house; I got to run down here. I will call you later today. She responded, okay. I put a couple of things and my suitcase, got dressed, and headed there. I called my best friend Winona; I told her William called and said Kendra shot herself. She responded, " That is ridiculous; I'm not surprised by all the stuff he has done to you and her. Why would she want to take her own life over him? She did it in his face to mess him up. Then I received a text message from Jessica, something to the fact don't tell anyone Kendra is dead or Kendra killed herself. I started crying and screaming; why would you let this man take you there to take your life? Why would you do that? She had two daughters. He deserved to have that type of trauma. He called me to see how far; I was getting on the highway, so I still had another 45 minutes. Please hurry, please hurry; I just can't believe this. He's crying on the phone, and I'm taking pity on him because he saw this traumatic event. I started thinking about my third daughter's father taking his own life. He called again to see how far I was. He was like, you know there's police everywhere here. They said something about the crime scene person coming. I just said I'm getting close; I'm getting close. Once I arrived and saw the police lights, it was surreal. I parked up the street and walked down the street; the First Responder worked the crime scene. I can't remember if the Medical Examiner was already there. Next door at his neighbor's house, I found him sitting on the step. Jessica was there walking around and crying; everybody was crying. I walked up to him, sat on the step, and hugged him. In my mind, I'm hugging this man who has caused this woman enough trauma to take her life, yet I am sitting here. I mentally disassociated myself as a fiancée and consoled him as I have done as an officer. I think to myself, what is he doing in town already? I'm supposed to be picking him up from the airport today. Not the time to bring that up or to discuss it. I looked up to the Medical Examiner removing her body from his townhouse; I cried. I had to get away from him for a moment. Jessica was at the corner of the neighbor's house throwing up. Another car pulled up, and I overheard Jessica say Kendra's people are here. I never saw their faces, but I knew more cars were there. I was trying to pay attention to everyone around me. I cannot remember the words, but he was mumbling stuff. The detective and the crime scene person needed to take photos of him. I walked over with him. I informed the detective I was in law enforcement and his fiancée. I saw them take photos of his hands and full body. She asked me to drive him to the police station for an interview. Maybe because I was law enforcement, she said it was okay to drive him. He was rocking back and forth in the seat. Once we arrived, she escorted us to her office. She explained that she was waiting for another person to arrive to assist her interview and transcribe his statement. The detective asked William which hand did Kendra have the gun? William stood up and demonstrated which hand (the left hand) and pointed to his head on the same side. I felt kind of out of place at that point. I don't need to be in here. She was concerned about him and wanted to get the interview done. He's rocking back and forth again. He kept grabbing, then holding the spot on his grey sweatpants near his knees. These were his favorite pair of sweatpants. He looked traumatized. I looked at him, thinking, you are responsible for all this pain. Kendra takes her life. I am sitting looking crazy and sick to the stomach. The person arrived to assist with the interview. I was sitting in the office by myself, and one of his relatives sent me a text asking what was going on but called me before I could respond. The detective was interviewing him. We leave the police station and go back to his house for some clothing items because the police had released the scene. The events began to move quickly, and my head was spinning again. I contacted my captain to inform him of the events happening. He suggested I take time off to help him with the trauma. I called Dr. Mitchell and asked if he could see William this evening? He scheduled an emergency counseling session, and I drove William to Atlanta. While we were traveling, he received a phone call from the detective requesting his sweatpants. I told him, no matter what, to make sure the detectives could reach him and know his whereabouts. While we were in the counseling session, Dr. Mitchell asked William questions, and he suddenly jumped up. He left out the room and disappeared. We finally located him outside of the building. I think he has PTSD. A few days later, a Bibb County police detective called me for an interview. I learned William lied to me about going to Dallas. I assumed he flew back early to surprise me. The detective learned William and I planned to get married on the 12th at the courthouse. He made the whole week up as if he was in Dallas and did not waiver. He sent me an email about a plane ticket to Dallas. I told him this was not an itinerary for an actual flight. I asked him whether he was out of town in Dallas. This man refused to answer my question. I stayed with William; I didn't deserve happiness. Kendra took her life from all the pain. I did want to be here anymore. I was weighing the options of taking my life. I didn't like disgracing my family. The situation with William and my job simultaneously equal I don't want to be here. The words, Are you going fix a temporary problem with a permanent solution? My children would not be able to handle it. My daughter

Aria lost one parent, and I would not do that to her. I wanted to meet my grandson, who was coming in July or August. I made an appointment with Behavioral Health at Kaiser Permanente. I was placed in an intensive group therapy session for six weeks, meeting three times a week. I think I cried for several days. The doctor prescribed medication that made me feel like a zombie. I started seeing blue spots everywhere and stopped taking medication. William led me to believe that he received death threats and needed my protection because he thought someone was following him. However, He did not need my protection for his birthday celebration; he would be the bruhs from his fraternity. He didn't think it was good for me to attend, so I headed home. His niece asked if I was coming to his birthday celebration for William. She said they would all be there along with his frat brothers. I acted as if I did not want to go, not knowing William had played it down to like a guys' night out. I learned that many people attended the gathering, including females. He enjoyed life, and the entire situation had me messed up. Kendra took her life dealing with him, and I am still here. It did not look good to stay with him when I looked back. I must understand the process God is taking me through and opening up my eyes. William manipulated the females in his family and me. Two of the three sisters told me I must stand by their brother because he was innocent. His now-deceased sister told me to make sure I care for my little brother. One sister revealed she had a conversation with William about choosing between Kendra and me. A niece said he didn't want me to know he was in town that week. Why were they telling me this stuff now? Back to reality. William said the ex-husband threatened to lock him up and throw away the key. I suggested he consult with a lawyer. He reached out to a fellow Omega man who gave him information and how much it would cost to retain him as his attorney. William gave me the money and asked me to meet with the attorney in Atlanta and pay him. Sgt Rutherford contacted me to come into her office about my statement on his case. William was so concerned about me meeting with her. I didn't think it was a big deal. Sgt. Rutherford has shown true concern and compassion about finding out the truth only. She informed me that the team had enough evidence and a warrant against William for the murder of Kendra. I broke down; she apologized and gave me some tissue to wipe my tears. I understood she had a job to do. She did not say anything further; she allowed me to get myself together before leaving her office. I was a sworn officer, and I have integrity. I felt it was not my job to inform William of their warrants. I am not sure why I was informed before they arrested him. I had nothing to do with his actions that night. When it crossed my mind years ago after I healed, I thought maybe it was a test to tell me and see my reactions afterward. I allowed the police to do their job. I did not have information or know the evidence, and it was not up to me. After leaving her office, I went to William's mom's house. He was very anxious and asked what she asked me. I told him she went over my statement for verification. Soon afterward, we had to go to his church in Perry. He knew something was on my mind, but I had to keep it together. What evidence did they have? What the hell did he do? Is he capable of this? After church, I told him I had to go back to Atlanta, and he insisted I go to dinner with him, but I refused. He was upset with me, but I didn't want to be there. He kept calling me to come back down, but I did want to see him. He said it was crazy there, and Sgt Rutherford was harassing people that knew him. I told him I could not come down because of my job, although I knew about the warrants. It was going on day four, and no arrest yet. In August 2015, I was at the hair salon when I received a phone call from Bibb County Sgt Rutherford's office, but William was on the phone. He asked whether I could call his lawyer and inform him of his arrest. His first appearance bond hearing was newsworthy and televised later that day on the news. The newspapers picked up the story from day one and continued to follow the case. I listened to the first appearance bond hearing on YouTube; Ms. Vicinda Crawford indicated they were to be married near the shooting date. He changed his story about the incident six different times. His first lawyer died in a one-car accident in Atlanta before his official trial. Everything completely derailed no longer employed as a DeKalb County police lieutenant. Four days later, A security company hired me as a security operations manager. I was in major depression and did not care about what happened to me. I separated myself from him. October 22, he was released on a $500,000 bond. I did not know he was also on house arrest. He kept calling me to come back because he loved me. He wanted me to marry him now. I told him I could not come around him. I said I would support him from afar. He keeps sending me emails and begging me to come back to him. I told him the first proposal did not count without a ring. On November 17, he officially proposed but with a ring. He took me with him to meet his second lawyer and his team. I did not think I should be there because it did not have anything to do with me. However, I supported him because he said they were setting him up in my head. Kendra's ex-husband, who was in law enforcement, was getting him back for taking Kendra and breaking up their family. The holidays passed through, and we were on to the new year. I separated ways from the security company on Christmas day. Starting the new year off unemployed and a full-time student. I sunk deeper into depression. Some days I did want to face the world. Ending my life crossed my mind daily, fighting mentally to stay in this world. No one knew what I was battling, and deep down, I felt they didn't care anyway. I was living off my college refund and waiting on my tax returns. I needed to find a job and keep my straight A in college. All my adult life, I was a police officer. Then In January or February 2016, he tore his Achilles and had major surgery. Yes, I went to help him heal. His surgery was a success, but I was in college full time and needed to go to class. He made me feel guilty about going to school and leaving him home. I wrote out the itinerary for the times and amount of medication he was supposed to take while I was in class. On the second week of his recovery, he told me his best friend was coming to see him. I set everything up before going to class and returned the next day. When I came into the house, something did not feel right. I guess the sixth sense does work. I could sense a woman had been there. I saw a fruit basket and other items. He assured me that his best friend had visited him. I did not say anything to him. His best friend came by two days later with a fruit basket. as she visited with us, she spoke about seeing

William for the first time in weeks. I am gradually starting to see his pattern. The biggest problem was I got in my head and excused things away. I needed to understand why he needed me in his life now. He went from wanting to get married immediately, so let's wait to see what happens. I spent a lot of time cleaning, washing clothes, working on my schoolwork, and traveling back and forth to Atlanta. He did not talk about the situation. He watched sports, played games on his phone, or texted unknown people. Once I lost my job in law enforcement, I noticed that he started changing toward me. I realized my being back started opening my eyes to stuff I refused to see. How the family helped with his manipulation. He told me his mother said I came back because I was trying to get information to take back to the prosecutor. What does he have to hide if she thinks that of me? He violated his bond by attending an Omega masquerade event in March and sending him back to jail. I found out the dynamics of his bond. He asked me to take care of the child support payments with his money. I contacted the child support office and obtained and mailed the money orders for the mothers. I realized he was not being honest with his lawyer about minor details of his whereabouts now. If you can lie to your defense attorney, something is wrong with you. Your family has helped you obtain the best lawyer in central Georgia. I knew it was time to remove myself from the situation. On December 15, they announced the indictment for the charge of malice murder, aggravated assault, and felony murder. I advised the family not to contact me about William. I sent them a copy of our agency policy advising that it was against policy to associate with anyone under indictment. I didn't want to be around him anymore. My eyes were finally wide open. I could see what everyone else saw in him. I felt bad that I went back to him. I thought, is this what Kendra went through? Was her mind manipulated like mine? Why did I love him so much? He bonded again after his first violation, but he had more restrictions. Nothing stopped him from pursuing me, sending emails with different love songs attached, which I ignored. He called my job, pretending to be his nephew with the attempts to speak with me. He had different people call my job to convince me to return to him. I texted his sister and gave specific instructions to tell William not to contact me directly or indirectly. Of course, William did not listen and continued to send emails. I contacted his attorney's office with my concerns and needed William to stop contacting me. He finally stopped sending emails. Then I found out he violated his bond again and returned to jail. He started sending letters from the jail to my house. I contacted the investigator and emailed all his letters to her. I was in my last class before I completed my bachelor's degree. It has been a long road, but I have maintained my straight A's. I received a direct message from Wanda asking me to attend her cousin's wedding on September 16. I was confused because I had no contact with the family. Why did you want me at the wedding? It was not fair to the bride on her special day. Although I thought something was not right, I agreed to attend. Why did the family want to see me? That answer came the next day. It had been two years since Kendra's death when the District Attorney's office contacted me. The victim advocate wanted to send me a subpoena to meet with the Assistant District Attorney (ADA) about the case. Per Williams's wishes, the family wanted to get in my head about the case before the ADA office contacted me. I could not understand what I would bring to his case. I told the victim advocate not to send a subpoena because I would come to the office on the needed date and time. William was still manipulating his family to get to me. I met with the ADA prosecutors and felt like shit. I felt punished for going back to him after the incident. I did not have any information, and William never confessed anything to me. They made me feel so stupid for trusting him. I had nothing to do with what happened that night. I have been very upfront and honest throughout the process. I hated William for bringing me into this mess from day one. I was mad at myself for believing him. I am thankful I finally opened my eyes to all his lies. I received notice the trial started in two weeks; however, they delayed the case. Sgt Rutherford was present when I met with the ADA prosecutors for more questioning. They treated me better than in the first interview. As a police officer, I understood their treatment as a hostile witness because I went back to him. The question: Was I loyal to him or loyal to the truth. I am loyal to the truth. I sent all the text messages between Kendra and me from May 31 conversation. The date was set for me to testify on October 20, 2017. This day was the anniversary of my kidney donation 14 years prior. I was at peace and knew God lined this day up for me. Thinking back to the morning 14 years ago. On October 20, 2003, the anesthesiologist instructed me to close my eyes and count backward from 100; I counted back to 98 and then drifted into a deep sleep. I made the ultimate and final decision to become a living donor. It was a final determination because the doctor asked me on the operation table if I still wanted to go through with the kidney donation. As a donor, you can change your mind before the anesthesiologist puts you to sleep. My journey with this decision began five months before surgery day. Here is my story! On a Tuesday afternoon in May 2003,

I received a phone call from the captain of the Homeland Security Division in the DeKalb County Police Department. She informed me of my reassignment to a new position as the Administrative Officer to Assistant Chief M. Eddison with DeKalb County Homeland Security Division. On Wednesday, she introduced me to Asst. Chief Eddison and I received my responsibilities for my new assignment. The end of the week was here; I uttered TGIF's famous words to Regina Longs, the Administrative Assistant, as she sat at her desk typing a memo. Asst. Chief Eddison rushed out of the office in a hurry with a distressed look on his face. Ms. Longs enlightened me with the sad news that Asst. Chief Eddison's son. Merlin Eddison, thirty-five years old, had been to the hospital for kidney failure. In my new position, one duty is to drive Asst. Chief Eddison around to different locations. The following Monday, Asst. Chief Eddison needed a ride to pick up Merlin from the dialysis center. Merlin was sick and unable to drive his vehicle back home. He spoke so proudly about Merlin and all the great things he has accomplished as a GBI agent. I thought to myself that God gave us two kidneys for a reason. It was to share an organ with someone in need one day. I told Chief that I would give him a kidney if I matched. The real journey began with several phone calls inquiring; what is required to become a living donor? First question, "What is your blood type?" The hospital sent four empty blood vials to collect my blood and start the process of elimination. In July 2003, the nurse who managed Merlin's donor process telephoned. Her voice was soft like a shy child on the first day at a new school. I heard the words, "Ms. Crawford, you are a match to give Merlin a kidney." I do not remember hanging up the phone or walking downstairs to Ms. Longs. She asked, "Are you okay?" I kept repeating softy and slowly- I am a match to Merlin. Asst. Chief Eddison was two rooms away from us, but with his bionic ear, he overheard my statement. He quickly jumped out of his chair and rushed out of the office with the biggest smile. Between July 17 and July 18, 2003, they poked, probed, and questioned the doctors, nurses, and psychologists to ensure I was physically and mentally healthy enough to donate a kidney. I was so exhausted by the end of the two days; I thought the doctors wanted both kidneys. The only process left was approval from the committee. On September 6, 2003, I celebrated my 37th birthday. On and about September 9, 2003, the telephone rang, and on the other side of the receiver was the soft voice of Merlin's managing nurse. She whispered the committee had approved the kidney transplant surgery. On Sunday, October 19, 2003, I arrived at Piedmont Hospital to prep for the big day. I met Merlin's beautiful wife, Toni, for the first time. She overcame emotions and thanked me for saving her husband's life. After my family and friends left the hospital, I prayed and went to bed. I was wheeled down to the operation's room and met with the anesthesiologist. The doctors went through the procedures again. The anesthesiologist instructed me to close my eyes and count backward from 100; I counted back to 98 and then drifted into a deep sleep. Our kidney donation story appeared on December 15, 2003, in JET magazine, on Channel 5 news, and on DeKalb County TV channel 22. The lifespan of a donated kidney average between 10 to 12 years. In 2014 I received a phone call from Merlin telling me he was back in the hospital. After 11 years, I learned my kidney has failed; he is again on dialysis but in high spirits. He told me I gave him the best years of his life to participate in his children's active sports lives freely. The rest is history. I knew I could not bring Kendra back, but I could testify.

My best friends Winona and Denise, my daughter Cortney and sister Renee traveled to Macon to support me. I was greeted by the prosecution team differently today. They smiled and were happy to see me. I was sitting in the lobby by myself when I noticed a black male attempting to contact me. I did not recognize him. The ADA could sense my nervousness and moved me into a glass room, asking the black male not to speak with me.

I hear my name called to come inside the courtroom. My eyes followed the bailiff as I walked behind him. I didn't want to see William. The courtroom setting where the defendant was behind you, facing the jury. I felt at ease, never having to see his face. I looked out into the courtroom and noticed a handful of people sitting on the defense side. The prosecution side was packed. Most of the people on the defense side were law students who came to observe his defense attorney. I was asked three to four questions from the prosecution side, but the focus was our text message conversation. I was able to give Kendra a voice through the text messages. To my surprise, the defense attorney only asked three questions. The victim advocate motioned me to sit down in the courtroom next to her. The judge called for a recess and dismissed everyone from the courtroom. I exited the courtroom and rested against the wall as the jurors walked through the lobby.

I found myself surrounded by William's family members. They were attempting to hug me. I could not handle it because some of the same people stood by while he conducted himself with Kendra and me. I was mentally exhausted from everything my body could not take anymore, and I went limped as my best friends caught me. I lost control of my emotion and broke down crying so hard, then pulled into the elevator and out of the building. I was still crying when I noticed a familiar slow down next to me as I was pacing outside my vehicle. It was the same guy from the lobby. I remembered his car and realized it was William's friend. He asked to speak with me and made it clear he was not a friend but wanted to see William get what he deserved. He expressed he wanted to tell me to run from William. He wished me blessings and drove away. I accidentally locked my keys in my vehicle before the court with all the stress. I had to stay in Macon for an hour, waiting for roadside assistance to retrieve my keys. Testimony continued for several days, and then the verdict. After three hours of deliberation, he was found guilty of all charges. The judge referred to him as a charlatan and then sentenced him to LIFE WITHOUT THE POSSIBILITY OF PAROLE. Mental health is indisputable. I have healed with intense therapy with Kaiser Permanente Behavior Health therapist, mediation.